Frank Andrew Munsey

The Boy Broker

Or, among the kings of Wall Street

Frank Andrew Munsey

The Boy Broker
Or, among the kings of Wall Street

ISBN/EAN: 9783337015725

Printed in Europe, USA, Canada, Australia, Japan

Cover: Foto ©Suzi / pixelio.de

More available books at **www.hansebooks.com**

HERBERT RANDOLPH EMERGES FROM THE CELLAR IN WHICH HE HAS BEEN KEPT A PRISONER.

OR,

AMONG THE KINGS OF WALL STREET.

BY

FRANK A. MUNSEY.

NEW YORK:
FRANK A. MUNSEY & CO., Publishers, 81 Warren Street.
1888.

Press of Ferris Brothers
[illegible] Pearl Street, N. Y.

TO MY DEAR FATHER,

WHOSE RIGID NEW ENGLAND DISCIPLINE SEEMED TO ME AS A BOY SEVERE AND UNNECESSARY, THIS VOLUME IS AFFECTIONATELY DEDICATED WITH THE GRATEFUL ACKNOWLEDGMENT THAT HE WAS RIGHT AND THAT I WAS WRONG. FOR THIS TRAINING AND FOR ALL ELSE I OWE HIM I CAN PAY THE DEBT BEST BY LIVING THE LIFE THAT WILL PLEASE HIM MOST.

PREFACE.

The best story for boys is the one that will help them most and give them the greatest pleasure—the story that will make them more manly, more self reliant, more generous, more noble and sweeter in disposition. Such a story I have aimed to make THE BOY BROKER. The moral or lesson it contains could be put into a very short lecture, but as a lecture I am confident that it would prove valueless. Boys are benefited little by advice. They seldom listen to it and less frequently make any practical application of it. Imitative by nature, they are easily influenced by those with whom they associate, and no associate, in my opinion, has so strong a grasp upon them as the hero of some much prized book. He becomes a real being to their young, healthy imagination—their ideal of manliness, bravery, generosity, and nobility. He enters into their lives, their sports, their adventures, their kind acts, a companion, a model so much idealized and admired that unconsciously they grow to be like him in so far as their surroundings will permit. In a good story plot and action are but the setting to the gem—the means of conveying a lesson in disguise in such a way that the reader will not suspect he is being taught. Let it once occur to him that he is reading a lecture and the book will at once be quietly but most effectually packed away. Many authors, it seems to me, fail in their purpose by devoting too much time to the gem and too little to the setting. Others go too far the other way and write stories that give young readers a wrong idea of life—stories whose heroes do improbable and unnatural acts. While my purpose has been to make THE BOY BROKER interesting I have aimed to give a true idea of life in a great city. So much nonsense of a misleading character has been written about benevolent old gentlemen who help poor boys from the country that I have sought to turn the light of fact on the subject and picture a little real life—about such life as a boy may expect to find if he comes to New York friendless and alone. He might find it much worse; he could not wisely hope to find it better.

FRANK A. MUNSEY.

NEW YORK, *September*, 1888.

LIST OF ILLUSTRATIONS.

THE GREAT CITY.

THE BOY BROKER.

CHAPTER I.

AN INTRODUCTION TO THE GREAT CITY.

"GIVE me the best morning paper you have, please."

"The *Tribune* costs the most, if that is the one you want."

"The price will be no objection providing the paper contains what I wish to find."

"You want work, I s'pose."

"Yes, I am looking for employment."

"I knew it—just in from the country too," said the newsboy, comically. "Well, what you want is the *Herald* or *World.* They are just loaded with wants."

"Thank you, you may give me both."

"Both! Whew, you must be well fixed!" replied the young metropolitan, handing over the papers, as he regarded his new customer curiously.

"What does that mean?" asked the latter, seriously.

"You don't know what well fixed means? You must have come from way back! Why it means—it means that you're solid, that you've got the stuff, don't you see?"

"I'm solid enough for a boy of my age, if that is the idea," replied the lad from the country, rather sharply, as a tinge of color rose to his cheeks.

"Shucks! That ain't the idea at all," said the street boy, in a tone that seemed apologetic. "What I mean is that you're a kind of boodle alderman—you're rich. Do you see now?"

"Oh! That's it. Well, you see, I didn't know what you meant. I never heard those terms up in Vermont. No; I'm not rich, but on the contrary have so little money that I must commence work at once."

"And that is why you bought two papers, so you can take in the whole business. You've got a big head, Vermont, any way, and would do stunnin' on mornin' papers."

"Thank you. Do you mean at selling them?"

"Yes, of course. You wouldn't give 'em away, would you?"

"Well, no, I should not be inclined to do so."

"That sounds more like it. Perhaps I'll give you a job, if you can't find anything else."

"Thank you, I may be very glad to get a chance to sell papers even."

"'Tain't a bad business anyhow. Me and lots of fellers makes plenty of money at it. But I s'pose you're hungry, hain't you? If you be I'll take you round to a boss place and it won't cost nothin' hardly."

"I am very much obliged to you, but I had my breakfast soon after leaving the boat."

"And I bet they done you up on the price. I tell you what it is, it takes a fellow a good while to learn to live in this city. You don't know nothin' about what it costs. Why I know a plenty of boys that spend more—yes, I'd say so, twice as much as what I do, and they don't throw no style into their livin' either. You see they don't know how and hain't got no taste, any way. But I like your looks, Vermont, and ef you want any points—and you're liable to want 'em in this city, I'll bet you—why you just call on me and I'll fix you out in big shape."

"YOU EVIDENTLY KNOW ALL ABOUT PROPRIETY, SO HERE IS MY HAND," SAID HERBERT.

"Thank you, sincerely," said the Green Mountain lad, a broad smile playing over his fine face, as he regarded the drollery of his new acquaintance. "I shall need many suggestions, no doubt, for I feel almost lost in this great city. I had no idea it was so large. I was never here before, and do not know where to go for a room or meals."

"So I thought, and that's why I offered to put you into the right track. My name is Bob Hunter—I hain't got no business cards yet, but all the boys knows me, and my place of business is right round here in City Hall Park. You'll find me here 'most any time durin' business hours."

"Bob Hunter! Well, you may be sure I shall remember your name and place of business, for I want to see you again. But what are your business hours?"

"Oh, yes; I forgot that. Everybody must have business hours, of course. Well, say from five to ten in the mornin', and three to eight in the afternoon, you can find me in."

"In! You mean *out*, don't you—out here?"

"Shucks! don't be so school mastery. Everybody in business says *in*. I guess I know what's proper!"

"All right, Bob Hunter, I'll give it up. You know all about propriety in New York, and I know nothing of it, so here is my hand. I'll say good by till tonight, when I will call upon you again. I must look over these papers now, and hunt for a situation."

"I hope you'll have luck, and get a bang up place. I'll be *in* when you call tonight; and if you hain't no objections, I'd like to know your name. It would be more handy to do business, you see. How could my clerks announce you so I'd know you, if I don't know your name? You see, I might think it was some one that wanted to collect a bill," continued Bob.

dryly, "and I'd be *out.* Don't you see how it's done? I'd just tell my clerks to say 'Mr. Hunter is not in;' so, you see, you would get left. Why, business men do it every day!"

"My name is Herbert Randolph," replied the other, laughing heartily at his comical friend—I say friend, for he already felt convinced that he had found one in Bob Hunter.

"Herbert Randolph! that's a tony name—some old fellow I read about in school was called Randolph; most likely he was some of your relations."

The day was too cold for him to remain out in the park and read; so Herbert, acting on the advice of Bob Hunter, hurried to the great granite post office, and there, in the rotunda, ran his eye over the "wants" in his two papers.

Many columns of closely printed matter in each paper offering every conceivable position were spread out before him—a bewildering display of flattering prospects.

Young Randolph soon learned that if he stopped to read every advertisement in both journals it would be very late in the day before he could apply for any position. But should he only read a few of the wants he might fail to notice the best openings. This was a misfortune, for he was ambitious to get the right position—the position that would enable him to advance the fastest; and like all inexperienced boys, he hoped and even expected he might get it the very first time trying.

He had already marked a dozen or two advertised situations which, it seemed to him, would do very well, in fact were quite desirable, but of course they were the high priced positions which would naturally be most sought after by thousands of other applicants—rivals whom the young Vermonter did not take into consideration. He saw before him a demand for four or five thousand people to help move the wheels of commerce.

He knew of course that he could only *accept* one position, so he was desirous that that one should be the best.

Any smart boy would feel as he did in this respect.

Some boys would even be so thoughtful of the interest of others as to feel sad that the four thousand nine hundred and ninety nine employers should be deprived of their services.

But young Randolph was more selfish. He had come here from the country with buoyant hopes and splendid courage. He proposed to make his way in New York—to become what is known as a successful man, to make a name for himself—a name that would extend to his native State and make his parents proud of their brilliant son.

Feeling thus, how natural it was that he should linger over the attractive columns much longer than was wise. Yet he did not think of this, or at least he did not give it any serious consideration, for were there not a vast number of positions to be filled? The question then was not whether he could get anything to do, but rather which one he should accept. When talking with young Bob Hunter, the newsboy, he had intimated that he might be glad even to get a chance to sell papers; but it must be remembered that he had not at that time seen a New York paper, and knew nothing of the tremendous demand for help.

Such a proposition from Bob now, however, would doubtless have been scorned, notwithstanding Herbert's usual good sense. And such scorn would have been very natural under the circumstances. Selling papers is an employment vastly inferior to clerking, to book keeping, to banking, to writing insurance policies, all of which positions were now open to him, as he supposed, else why should they be advertised? And why could not he fill them—any one of them? He was honest, ambitious, willing to work hard, wrote a splendid hand, had had some experience in clerking in a country store, and, best of all, he knew he would be faithful to his employer—all excellent qualifications in a general way—qualifications that probably seemed to him irresistible. Then, too, might he not lend a degree of intelligence, of thought to the business that would be helpful? This was a point that did not occur to him at first—not till his mind became inspired with the subject; but now the idea seemed to him a good one, and he wondered that he had not thought of it before. At any rate, he decided not to lose sight of it again, for he knew—his common sense told him, and he had read also, that the men who move things in this world are men of brains—men who *think*, who lend ideas to business, to inventions, to anything and everything with which they have to deal.

HERBERT RANDOLPH IN THE POST OFFICE.

Thus another complication was added, for now he must consider in determining if the position he accepted would give him the widest scope for thought, and the broadest play for genius, ideas, originality and enterprise. His imagination ran fast. He was dead to the busy scenes about him. Great questions pressed home upon him for decision, and he did not decide quickly and without thought, as a light headed boy would have done. No, he pondered long and hard over the subject which meant so much to him, and perhaps to the entire commerce of the city and even the finances of the nation. What might not grow out of his start in life—the start of a thoughtful, industrious, original man? How important, then, that it should be a right start! What might not come of a false venture? How the possibilities of the future might be dwarfed by such a move!

These were momentous questions for this young ambitious boy to solve. He grappled with them bravely, and with flushed cheeks and dilated eyes knitted his brows and thought. He thought hard, thought as one with the responsibilities of a nation resting upon him—this young untried, untrained boy from old Vermont.

"No, I will not take it," he broke out suddenly and with striking determination in his face. "Simply because I write a good hand they would keep me writing policies all the time, and then I believe the insurance business is run like a big machine. No, I do not want it and will not take it, for I am not going to make a mistake this time. I want to show the folks down home who said I would make a failure here that they didn't *know me*—they counted on the wrong man. No, insurance is good enough for any one without ambition or ideas, who always wants to be a clerk, but I'm not that kind of a man."

He was actually calling himself a man now.

"But I think mercantile business or manufacturing or banking would do for me and would be suited to me. I wonder which is the best! Mercantile business gives one a good chance to show what he is made of. A man with ideas ought to succeed in it; that is, if he is pushing and has plenty of originality. A. T. Stewart, what a fortune he made! He was original, he did things in a new way, advertised differently, got up new ideas, and pushed his business with close attention. He started without any money. I have no money. He was a hard worker, a thinker, an originator, a pusher. Why shouldn't I be a hard worker, a thinker, an originator and a pusher? I think I will. But these qualifications will win just as well in the manufacturing and banking business as in mercantile pursuits, and if I have them I shall succeed anywhere. I wonder why those people in Vermont thought I would not succeed here. I wish they could see the chances I have.

"Well, I do not think I'll take to manufacturing, though here are a dozen or so first class situations in that line. I might like it well enough, but I believe banking would suit me better —that is, banking or the mercantile business, and I don't care much which. Of course banking will be easier at first than clerking, so I should have more time for thought and study—time to get right down to the science of the business. Yes, I believe I'll try banking. Here are four banks that want a young man. I'll take a look at each, for I want the best one."

Thus young Randolph reasoned, feeling no uneasiness about procuring a situation, though he had wasted in building foolish air castles so much valuable time that he had really almost no chance of obtaining a situation of any kind that day. This he learned to his sorrow a little later, when he commenced in earnest the very difficult undertaking of getting employment in a great city.

CHAPTER II.

AN EFFORT TO OBTAIN EMPLOYMENT.

WHAT a common occurrence it is for people to do foolish things. How often we see a man of education and broad influence—a hard headed man of sense, who has made his own way against stubborn opposition, and accumulated great wealth—how often, I say, we see such a man exhibit a degree of simplicity in money making or some other matter that would seem weak in an untutored boy. When he already has more money than he knows what to do with, he will perhaps hazard all on some wild cat speculation, and in a very little while find himself penniless and unable to furnish support for his family. Again he becomes the victim of a confidence game, and only learns how he has been played with when he has lost perhaps fifty thousand dollars by the unscrupulous sharpers with whom he has been dealing.

Such exhibitions of weakness in men to whom the community looks for an example are always surprising, always painful; but they teach us the important fact that human nature is easily influenced, easily molded, easily led this way or that when the proper influences are brought to bear upon it.

It is not so strange, then, that young Herbert Randolph, fresh from the country and as ignorant of the city as a native African, should have become dazzled by the flattering prospects spread out before him. What a busy city New York seemed to him when he landed from the boat in the early morning! Everything was bustle and activity. People were hurrying along the streets as he had never seen them move in his quiet country town. No idlers were about. Men and boys alike were full of business—they showed it in their faces, their every movement. These facts impressed the young country lad far more than the tall buildings and fine streets. His own active nature bounded with admiration at the life and dash on every hand. He had been reared among sleepy people—people in a rut, whose blood flowed as slowly as the sluggish current upon which they floated towards their final destiny.

But young Randolph was not of their class. He had inherited an active mind, and an ambition that made him chafe at his inharmonious surroundings at home. The very atmosphere, therefore, of this great city, laden with the hum of activity, was stimulating and even intoxicating to his boundless ambition. He had been a great reader. Biography had been his favorite pastime He knew the struggles and triumphs of many of our most conspicuous merchant princes. Not a few familiar names, displayed on great buildings which towered over the tops of their smaller neighbors, greeted his eyes as he approached the city by boat, and passed through the streets after landing. These sights were food for his imagination. He compared himself, his qualifications, his poverty, and his opportunities for advancement in this world of activity with the advent into New York of the men he had taken as models for his own career. There was in a general way a striking likeness between the two pictures as he viewed them. Their struggles had been so long and fierce that it seemed to him they must have been made of iron to finally win the fight.

Yet these very difficulties lent attractiveness to the picture. They made heroes of his models, whose example he burned with enthusiasm to follow. Thus it will be seen that in the early morning he expected to meet bitter discouragements, to encounter poverty in its most depressing form, and to meet rebuffs on the right hand and on the left. He expected all this. He rather craved it from the sentimental, heroic standpoint, because the men he had chosen to follow had been compelled to force their way through a similar opposition.

From this view of the boy it is plain that he was sincere in thanking young Bob Hunter, a little later, for the newsboy's generous offer to take him into the paper trade. But a little later still, when he enters the post office and becomes intoxicated with the sudden, the unexpected, the overwhelming opportunities displayed before him—the urgent demands, even, for his services in helping to push forward the commerce of this vast city, he presents himself in an entirely new light. His head has been turned. He has lost sight of the early struggles of his heroes, and now revels in the brilliant pictures drawn by his imagination. How flattering to himself are these airy, short lived fabrics, and how sweet to his young ambition!

Had young Randolph been an ordinary boy of slow intellect, he would never have indulged in these beautiful dreams, which to the stupid mind would seem silly and absurd, but to him were living realities—creations to beckon him on, to encourage him in the hours of danger and to sustain him in the stern battle before him.

Did he then waste his time in what would seem wild imagination, when a more practically minded boy would have been applying for work? Yes, in the smaller sense, he idled his time away; but in the broader, he builded better than he knew.

To be sure, he had lost the opportunity of securing a situation on that day—and he needed work urgently—but he had fixed upon *an ideal*—a standard of his own, to be the goal of all his efforts and struggles. And such an ideal was priceless to him. It would prove priceless to any boy, for without lofty aims no young man can ever hope to occupy a high position in life.

Of course he appears foolish in forgetting what he had anticipated, namely the difficulties he would in all probability experi-

MEMORIES OF COUNTRY LIFE—THE GREETING BY THE WAY.

ence in finding a situation, but the fact that five thousand positions were offered to him who knew nothing of the tremendous demand for such situations entirely deluded him. Once forgetting this important point, his mind ran on and on, growing bolder and bolder as thought sped forward unrestrained in wild, hilarious delight.

What pleasure in that half hour's thought—sweet, pure, intoxicating pleasure, finer and more delicate than any real scene in life can ever afford.

But everything has a price, and that price must many times be paid in advance. Those delightful moments passed in thinking out for himself a grand career cost young Randolph far more than he felt he could afford to pay. They cost him the opportunity of securing a position on that day, and made him sick at his own ignorance and folly. He felt ashamed of himself and disgusted at his stupidity, as he walked block after block with tired feet and heavy heart, after being coldly turned away from dozens of business houses with no encouragement whatever. He went from banking to mercantile pursuits, then to insurance, to manufacturing, and so on down, grade after grade, till he would have been glad to get any sort of position at honest labor. But none was offered to him and he found no opening of any sort.

Night was coming on. He was tired and hungry. His spirits ran low. In the post office in the early part of the day they soared to unusual height, and now they were correspondingly depressed. What should he do next? Where should he spend the night? These questions pressed him for an answer. He thought of Bob Hunter, and his cheeks flushed with shame. He would not have the newsboy know how foolish he had been to waste his time in silly speculation. He knew the young New Yorker would question him, and he would have to hide the real cause of his failure, should he join his friend. He was fast nearing Bob's place of business, and he decided to stop for a few moments' reflection, and to rest his weary limbs as well. Accordingly he stepped to the inner side of the flagging and rested against the massive stone base of the Astor House.

Looking to his right Broadway extended down to the Battery, and to his left it stretched far away northward. Up this famous thoroughfare a mighty stream of humanity flowed homeward. Young Randolph watched the scene with much interest, forgetting for a time his own heavy heart. Soon, however, the question what to do with himself pressed him again for an answer. How entirely alone he felt! Of all the thousands of people passing by him, not one with a familiar face. Every one seemed absorbed in himself, and took no more notice of our country lad than if he had been a portion of the cold inanimate granite against which he stood. Herbert felt this keenly, for in the country it was so different. There every one had a kind look or a pleasant word for a fellow man to cheer him on his way.

CHAPTER III.

AN EVENING WITH BOB HUNTER.

CHILLY from approaching night and strengthening wind, and depressed by a disheartening sense of loneliness and a keen realization of failure on the first day of his new career, Herbert felt homesick and almost discouraged.

At length he joined the passers by, and walked quickly until opposite City Hall Park. He crossed Broadway and soon found himself at young Bob Hunter's "place of business." The latter was "in," and very glad he seemed to see his new friend again. His kindly grasp of the hand and hearty welcome acted like magic upon Herbert Randolph; but his wretchedly disheartened look did not change in time to escape the keen young newsboy's notice.

"Didn't strike it rich today, did you?" said he, with a smile.

"No," replied Herbert sadly.

"Didn't find no benevelent old gentleman—them as is always looking for poor boys to help along and give 'em money and a bang up time?"

"I did not see any such philanthropist looking for me," answered Herbert, slightly puzzled, for the newsboy's face was seriousness itself.

"Well, that is all fired strange. I don't see how he missed you, for they takes right to country boys."

"I did not start out very early," remarked Herbert doubtfully, and with heightened color.

"Then that's how it happened, I guess," said Bob, with a very thoughtful air. "But you must have found somebody's pocket book——"

"What do you mean?" interrupted Herbert suspiciously.

"Mean — why what could I mean? Wasn't it plain what I said? Wasn't I speaking good English, I'd like to know?" said Bob, apparently injured.

THE BENEVOLENT OLD GENTLEMAN PRESSES MONEY ON THE COUNTRY BOY.

"Your language was plain, to be sure, and your English was good enough," apologized Herbert; "but I can't see why I should find anybody's pocket book."

"Jest what I thought, but you see you don't know the ways of New York. You will learn, though, and you will be surprised to see how easy it is to pick up a pocket book full of greenbacks and bonds—perhaps a hundred thousand dollars in any one of 'em—and then you will take it to the man what lost it, and he will give you a lots of money, maby a thousand dollars or so—'twouldn't be much of a man as would do less than a thousand. What do you think?"

"I don't know what to think. I cannot understand you, Bob Hunter."

"That's 'cause you don't know me, and ain't posted on

what I'm saying. Maby I am springin' it on you kinder fresh for the first day, though I guess you will stand it. But tell me, Vermont, about the runaway horse that you stopped."

"The runaway horse that I stopped!" exclaimed Herbert. "You must be mad to talk in this way."

"Mad! Well, that's good; that's the best thing I've heard of yet! Do I look like a fellow that's mad?" and he laughed convulsively, much to the country lad's annoyance.

"No, you do not look as if you were mad, but you certainly act as if you were," replied the latter sharply.

"Now look a here, Vermont, this won't do," said Bob, very serious again. "You are jest tryin' to fool me, but you can't do it, Vermont, I'll tell you that straight. Of course I don't blame you for wantin' to be kinder modest about it, for I s'pose it seems to you like puttin' on airs to admit you saved their lives. But then 'tain't puttin' on no airs at all. Ef I was you I'd be proud to own it; other boys always owns it, and they don't show no modesty about it the same as what you do, either. And I don't know why they should, for it's something to be proud of; and you know, Vermont, the funniest thing about it is that them runaways is always stopped by boys from the country jest like you. Don't ask me why it happens so, for I don't know myself; but all the books will tell you that it is so. And jest think, Vermont, how many lives they save! You know the coachman gets paralyzed, and the horses runs away and he tumbles off his box, and a rich lady and her daughter—they are always rich, and the daughter is always in the carriage, too—funny, ain't it, but it's as true as I'm alive; and the boy rushes at the horses when they are going like a cyclone, and stops 'em jest as the carriage is going to be dashed to pieces. And then the lady cries and throws her arms round the boy, and kisses him, and puts a hundred dollars in his hands, and he refuses it. Then the lady and her daughter ask him to come up to their house, and the next day her husband gets a bang up position for him, where he can make any amount of money.

THE COUNTRY BOY FINDS A WELL FILLED POCKET BOOK.

"Now I call that somethin' to be proud of, as I said before, and I don't see no sense in your tryin' to seem ignorant about it. Why, I wouldn't be surprised a bit ef you would try to make out that you wasn't anear any fire today. But that wouldn't do, Vermont—I'll give you a pointer on that now, so you won't attempt no such tomfoolery with me, for no boy like you ever comes into a town like New York is and don't save somebody from burning up—rescue 'em from a tall building when nobody else can get to 'em. And of course for doing this they get pushed right ahead into something fine, while us city fellows have to shin around lively for a livin'.

"I don't know

ef you saved anybody from drowning or not; I won't say that you did, but ef you didn't you ain't in luck, that's all I've got to say about it. So you see 'taint much use for you to try to deceive me, Vermont, for I know jest what's a fair day's work for a boy from the country—jest what's expected of him on his first day here. Why, ef you don't believe me (and I know you don't by the way you look), jest get all the books that tells about country boys coming to New York, and read what they say, that's all I ask of you, Vermont. Now come, own up and tell it straight."

"Bob, you are altogether too funny," laughed Herbert, now that the drift of his friend's seemingly crazy remarks was plain to him. "How can you manage to joke so seriously, and why do you make fun of me? Because I am from the country, I suppose."

"I hope I didn't hurt your feelings, Vermont," replied Bob, enjoying greatly his own good natured satire.

"No, not at all, Bob Hunter, but until I saw your joke I thought surely you were insane."

"Well, you see, I thought you needed something to kinder knock the blues that you brought back with you tonight—'tain't much fun to have 'em, is it? Sometimes I get 'em myself, so I know what they're like. But now to be honest, and not fool no more, didn't you get no show today?"

"No, not the least bit of encouragement," replied Herbert.

"And you kept up the hunt all day?"

"Yes."

"I ought ter told you that that wan't no use."

"How is that?"

"Why, don't you see, it's the first fellers what gets the jobs—them as gets round early."

"And are there so many applicants for every position?"

"Are there? Well, you jest bet there are. I've seen more'n two hundred boys after a place, and 'twan't nothin' extra of a place, either."

"But then there are thousands of places to be filled. Why, the papers were full of them."

"Yes, and there is a good many more thousands what wants them same jobs. You never thought of that, I guess."

Herbert admitted with flushed cheeks that he had not given that fact proper consideration.

"Well, you done well, any way, to hang on so long," said Bob, in his off hand, comical manner. "I expected you'd get sick before this time, and steer straight for Vermont."

"Why did you think that?"

"Well, most of the country boys think they can pick up money on the streets in New York; but when they get here, and begin to hunt for it, they tumble rather spry—I mean they find they've been took in, and that a fellow has got to work harder, yes, I'd say so, ten times harder, here'n he does on a farm. There he can just sleep and laze round in the sun, and go in swimmin', and all the time the stuff is just growin' and whoopin' her right along, like as if I

THE COUNTRY BOY TO THE RESCUE.

was boss of a dozen boys, and they was all sellin' papers and I was makin' a profit on 'em all, and wasn't doin' nothin' myself. So when these fellers find out they've got to knuckle down and shine shoes, why they just light out kinder lively, and make up their minds that New York ain't much of a town no how."

"And so you thought I would 'light out' too," laughed Herbert.

"Well, I didn't know. I told you I liked your looks, but I hain't much faith in nobody till I know what kind of stuff a feller is made of. But if he's got any sand in him, then I'll bet on his winning right here in New York, and he won't have to go back home for his bread. Well, speakin' of bread reminds me that it's about time to eat somethin', and I'm all fired hungry, and you look es ef 'twould do you good to get a little somethin' warm in your stomach. Funny, ain't it, we can't do nothin' without eatin'? But we can't, so let's eat. Business is about over, and I don't mind leavin' a little early, any way."

Herbert assented gladly to this proposition, and presently Bob took him up Chatham Street to an eating house known as the "Boss Tweed Restaurant"—a restaurant the cheapness of which recommended it, five cents being the established price for a meal.

"I s'pose you hain't made no plans for a place to sleep yet?" said the newsboy, while eating their frugal fare.

"No," replied Herbert. "I thought I would wait and see you before making any move in that direction. You are the only one I know in the city."

"And 'tain't much you know about me."

"Very true; but from your appearance I'm satisfied to trust myself with you."

"You're takin' big chances ef you do," replied Bob, happily; "but ef you want to take the resk, why we will jest look up a room and occupy it together. I kinder think I'd like the scheme. I've been sleepin' at the Newsboys' Lodging House, but I'm tired of it. What do you say?"

"I say yes," replied Herbert. He was only too glad of the chance, and liked the idea of having Bob Hunter for a room mate. He thought there would be something fascinating about living with a newsboy, and learning this phase of life in a great city, especially when the newsboy was so droll as Bob Hunter had already shown himself to be.

AT THE BOSS TWEED RESTAURANT.

"All right, then, it's a go," replied Bob, greatly pleased.

When the meal had been finished they continued up Chatham Street into the Bowery, and then turned into a side street where inexpensive rooms were offered for rent. After a little hunting they found one at a cost of one dollar a week which proved satisfactory. They immediately took possession, and went to bed very early, as Herbert was practically worn out.

CHAPTER IV.

AT MR. GOLDWIN'S OFFICE.

ON the following morning both boys rose early and breakfasted together. Then Bob hurried away to his paper trade, and Herbert applied himself diligently to reading the "wants." The following advertisement especially attracted his attention:

> WANTED, a bright, smart American boy of about sixteen years of age; must have good education, good character, and be willing to work. Salary small, but faithful services will be rewarded with advancement.
> RICHARD GOLDWIN,
> Banker and Broker, Wall Street.

"I think I can fill those requirements," said young Randolph to himself, thoughtfully. "For all I can see, I am as likely to be accepted by a banker as a baker or any one else in want of help. There will doubtless be a lot of applicants for the position, and so there would if the demand was for street cleaning, therefore I think I may as well take my chances with the bank as at anything else."

Having come to this conclusion, he talked the matter over with Bob Hunter, upon whose practical sense Herbert was beginning to place a high value. The shrewd young newsboy approved of the plan, so our country lad started early for Wall Street, where the great money kings are popularly supposed to hold high carnival, and do all sorts of extraordinary things. When he arrived, however, at Richard Goldwin's banking house, his hopes sank very low, for before him was a long line of perhaps forty or fifty boys, each of whom had come there hoping to secure the advertised position.

This crowd of young Americans comprised various grades of boys. Some were stupid, others intelligent; a few were quiet and orderly, but the majority were boisterous and rough. Squabbling was active, and taunts and jeers were so numerous, that a strange boy from a quiet country home would have hardly dared to join this motley crowd, unless he was possessed of rare courage and determination.

Herbert Randolph paused for a moment when he had passed through the outer door, and beheld the spectacle before him. He wondered if he had made a mistake and entered the wrong place; but before he had time to settle this question in his own mind, one of the boys before him, who was taller and more uncivil than those about him, and seemed to be a leader among them, shouted, derisively:

A GLIMPSE OF WALL STREET.

"Here's a new candidate—right from the barnyard too!"

All turned their attention at once to the object of the speaker's ridicule, and joined him in such remarks as "potato bug," "country," "corn fed," "greeny," "boots," and all the time they howled and jeered at the boy from the farm most unmercifully.

"You think you'll carry off this position, maybe," said the leader, sarcastically. "You'd better go home and raise cabbage or punkins!"

Again the crowd exploded with laughter, and as many mean things as could be thought of were said. Herbert made no reply, but instead of turning back and running away from such a crowd, as most boys would have done, he stepped forward boldly, and took his place in the line with others to await the arrival of the banker.

His face was flushed, and he showed plainly his indignation at the insolent remarks made to him. Nevertheless, this very abuse stimulated his determination to such a degree, that he was now the last boy in the world to be driven away by the insults and bullying of those about him.

His defiance was so bold, and his manner was so firm and independent, that he at once commanded the respect of the majority of the long line of applicants, though all wished he were out of the way; for they saw in him a dangerous rival for the position they sought.

A notable exception, however, to those who shared this better feeling, was the boy whom I have spoken of as the "leader," for such he seemed to be. He was no ordinary boy, this bright, keen, New York lad, with a form of rare build, tall and straight as a young Indian. He showed in every movement, and in the manner of his speech, that his character was a positive one, and that nature had endowed him with the qualities of a leader.

HERBERT RANDOLPH FINDS HIMSELF AMONG A MOB OF RIVAL APPLICANTS.

These gifts he now exercised with remarkable effect upon the raw material about him, if by such a term I may characterize the peculiarly mixed crowd of boys in line.

When, however, Herbert Randolph advanced to his position with such unmistakable determination in his manner, and with firmness so distinctly showing in every muscle of his face, our young leader trembled visibly for an instant, and then the hot blood mantling his cheeks betrayed his anger.

He had endeavored to drive away the young Vermonter by jeers and bullying, but he failed in this attempt. In him he found his match—a boy quite equal to himself in determination, in the elegance of his figure and the superiority of his intellect.

The country boy lacked, however, the polish and grace of the city, and that ease and assurance that comes from association with people in large towns. But the purity of his character, a character as solid as the granite hills of his native State, was of infinitely more value to him than was all the freedom of city manner to the New York lad.

These two boys were no ordinary youths. Each of them possessed a positive and determined character. The one was bold as the other, and in intellect and the commanding qualities of their minds they were giants among boys.

The others felt this now in the case of both, as they had but a few moments before felt it regarding the one. They realized their own inferiority. The jeering and bullying ceased, and all was quiet, save the slam of the door, as new applicants now and then dropped in and joined the line. The silence became painful as the two prominent figures eyed each other. Herbert knew better than to make the first move. He waited the action of his rival, ready to defend his position.

The strange and sudden quiet of all the boys, who had but a few moments before been so noisy and insulting, gave him renewed courage. He saw, to his great relief, that he had but one mind to contend with—but one enemy to overcome. In this one's face, however, was pictured a degree of cunning and anger that he had never seen before in all his simple life.

The evil designs in the face of the city boy momentarily became more noticeable. Why had he so suddenly stopped his derisive remarks? And why should he show his evident hatred toward our hero? Is it possible that he dare not attack him, and that he is afraid to continue the bullying further? That he feels that Herbert is his equal, and perhaps more than a match for him, seems evident; and yet he will not acknowledge himself inferior to any one, much less to this country lad.

"No, he *shall not* get this situation away from me," he said determinedly to himself; and then his mind seemed bent upon some deep plot or wicked scheme.

CHAPTER V.

THE CONTEST BETWEEN HERBERT AND FELIX.

PRESENTLY the inner doors of the banking house were thrown open, and a gentleman of perhaps a little more than middle age stepped lightly into the corridor, where the boys awaited his arrival. He had a kindly face, and a sharp but pleasant blue eye.

All seemed to know intuitively that he was Richard Goldwin, the banker, and consequently each one made a dashing, but somewhat comical effort to appear to good advantage.

"Good morning, boys," said the banker, pleasantly, "I am glad to see so many of you here, and I wish I was able to give each one of you a position. I see, however, that many of you are too young for my purpose; therefore it would be useless to waste your time and mine by further examination."

In a little time the contest had narrowed down to but two, and they were Herbert Randolph, and the boy who had so ineffectually attempted to drive him away.

"What is your name?" asked the banker of the city lad.

"My name is Felix Mortimer."

"Felix Mortimer?"

"Yes, sir."

"Mortimer, Mortimer," repeated Mr. Goldwin. "The name sounds familiar, but I can't place it. Do you live in New York?"

"Yes, sir."

"In what part of the city?"

"In Eleventh Street, sir—on the East Side."

"Well, you appear like a bright boy. Are you ambitious to work your way up in a solid, reliable business?"

"Yes, sir, I am; and banking is just what I would like."

"And you are willing to work hard?"

"Yes, sir, I think I could satisfy you that I am."

"What is your age?"

"I am seventeen years old."

"Have you ever worked in any business house?"

"Yes, I have had two years' experience in business."

"You commenced rather young—so young that I am afraid your education was neglected."

"Well, I was a good scholar in school; here is a recommendation from my teacher."

Richard Goldwin read the letter, which purported to be signed by the principal of a well known school.

"This speaks well of you," said the banker.

Felix looked pleased, and cast a triumphant glance at Herbert, who sat at a little distance off, anxiously awaiting his turn to be examined. He was afraid the banker might settle upon young Mortimer without even investigating his own fitness for the position.

"For what firm did you work?" asked Richard Goldwin.

"For Wormley & Jollup," replied Felix, firmly.

"The large trunk manufacturers up Broadway?"

"Yes, sir."

"Why didn't you remain with them?"

This question would have confused some boys, had they been in the place of Felix; but it did not affect him in the slightest degree, though the keen and practiced eye of the banker watched him closely.

"Why, don't you remember that Wormley & Jollup had a big strike in their factory?"

"Yes, the papers printed a great deal about it."

"Well, you see, they couldn't get any trunks made; so business got dull in the store."

"They wouldn't give in to the strikers, I believe?"

"No; and the result was they had to let a lot of us go."

"It was an unfortunate affair. But I suppose you got a recommendation from Wormley & Jollup?"

"Yes, sir," said Felix, with all the assurance of one who was telling the truth; "there it is—signed by Mr. Jollup himself."

The letter was highly complimentary to Felix Mortimer.

"No one could ask for a better recommendation than this," said the banker, looking as if he thought he had found a prize in the boy before him.

Had he suspected that this very recommendation was forged, he would have been angry. Now, however, he felt quite the reverse; and decided to give Herbert a hearing more as a matter of courtesy than otherwise, for he had practically settled upon young Mortimer for the position in his banking house.

Felix saw this and could hardly restrain his happiness, as he saw pictured on the young Vermonter's face unmistakable discomfiture.

"Well, you may be seated," said Mr. Goldwin; "I wish to see what this young man has to say for himself before engaging any one."

"So you came from Vermont, right from the farm?" said the banker to Herbert, after a few minutes' conversation.

"Yes, sir," returned young Randolph.

"And I suppose you expect to make your fortune in this city?"

"I have not got so far along as that yet, sir. I hope, however, that I shall do well here."

"You look like a plucky lad, and those red cheeks of yours are worth a fortune. I remember well when mine were as full of rich young blood as yours are now. I was a country lad myself."

"Then your career shows that a boy from the country may make a success."

"Yes, that is very true. Many of our most successful men came from the farm; but I assure you, my boy, that success is not an easy thing to pick up in a big city. The chances are a hundred to one against any boy who comes here from the country. If, however, he does not succumb to temptation, and has sufficient pluck and perseverance, he can do well in this city."

"I am quite ready to take that hundredth chance," said Herbert, in a way that pleased the banker.

"Well, I admire your courage, young man, but now to return to business. Suppose I were to give you a situation, how could you live on three dollars a week? You say you have no means, and must earn your own living. I cannot pay a larger salary at first."

"I am sure I can manage that all right, sir; one can do what he must do."

"That is true; your ideas are sound there, surely. What is your age?"

"I am nearly seventeen, sir."

"You are so strongly built, perhaps you could get a place

where more money could be paid for your services; some place where heavy work is to be done."

"I am not afraid of hard work, for I have always been accustomed to it; but I would much rather have a chance where there are good prospects ahead."

"Again you are right," said the banker, now becoming interested in the young Vermonter. "What is your education?"

"I passed through our district school, and went for several terms to the Green Mountain Academy. I have taught three terms of school."

"Three terms! You certainly must have commenced young."

"Yes; I was not very old. I got my first school when I was fifteen."

"Do you write a good hand? Please come to this desk, and show me what you can do."

Herbert complied readily with the request, and was most happy to do so, for he had spent many hours in practicing penmanship, and now wrote a beautiful hand.

Richard Goldwin was surprised when he took up the sheet of paper and ran his eye over the well formed letters.

"Mr. Mortimer, will you please show me what you can do with the pen?" said the banker.

Felix rose to his feet, and the color rose to his face. He wasn't very powerful with the pen, and he knew it; but another matter disconcerted him. He feared, and well he might, that his writing would resemble, only too closely, that in the recommendation which he had shown to Mr. Goldwin. But he was equal to the emergency, and, to make the disguise perfect, he gave to his writing the left hand or backhand stroke. This was done at the expense of his penmanship, which, however, would not have been considered absolutely bad, had it not been compared with the gracefully and perfectly cut letters of Herbert Randolph.

The banker looked at both critically for a moment, and then, after a pause, said:

"Mr. Mortimer, I would like to speak with you alone."

The latter followed him to the outer office.

"Your manner pleases me, young man," said Mr. Goldwin, pleasantly, "and with one exception I see but little choice between you two boys, but that little is in your competitor's favor."

The color left Felix Mortimer's face.

"I refer," continued the banker, "to his penmanship, which you must acknowledge is far superior to your own; and a good handwriting adds much to one's value in an office of this sort. I see you are disappointed, and I knew you would be. Do not, however, feel discouraged, as it is possible I may do something for you yet. If Mr. Randolph should prove unsatisfactory in any respect, he will not be retained permanently. You may, therefore, if you choose, run in here again in a day or two."

Young Mortimer was greatly disappointed and even deeply chagrined, for he had supposed himself more than capable of holding his own against this unsophisticated country lad. Had he not attempted to bully him while waiting for the banker and failed, thus arousing a spirit of rivalry and hostility between young Randolph and himself, he would of course have felt differently, but now an intense hatred was kindled within him, and with burning passion he determined upon revenge.

Felix Mortimer went direct from Richard Goldwin's banking house to the Bowery, and from there he soon found his way to a side street, which contained many old buildings of unattractive appearance. The neighborhood was a disreputable one. Squalor was on every hand, and many individuals of unsavory reputations made this locality their headquarters. One of these was Christopher Gunwagner, a repulsive specimen of humanity, who had been in business here for several years as a "fence," or receiver of stolen goods.

To this fence Felix directed his steps.

"Good morning, Mr. Gunwagner," said young Mortimer, briskly.

The former eyed him sharply for a moment.

"What do you want now?" growled the fence by way of reply. "Why don't you bring me something, as you ought to?"

Felix cut him short, and at once proceeded to business.

"I came," said he, "to get you to help me and thereby help yourself. I've got a chance to get into a bank——"

"Into a bank?" interrupted Gunwagner, now interested.

"Yes."

"Where?"

"On Wall Street, in Richard Goldwin's banking house."

"If you don't take it, you're a fool. Goldwin's, hey?" he went on; "we can make it pay us; yes, yes, we are in luck." And he rubbed his thin hands together greedily.

"I expect to take it as soon as I can get it," said Felix; and then he described the competitive examination between himself and the young Vermonter.

"So you want to get him out of the way, eh?"

"You have struck it right this time. That's just what I want, and propose to do."

"And you expect me to help you?"

"Certainly I do. To whom else should I go?"

"What do you want me to do?"

"I haven't quite got the plan yet, and want your advice. You see if I can get him out of the way for a few days, so he won't show up, why old Goldwin will take me in his place. If I can once get in there, and remain till I get the run of things, we can have it our own way."

GUNWAGNER AND FELIX AGREE UPON A PLAN.

Gunwagner's face grew more and more avaricious. The plan looked well to him, and he felt it would be a great thing to have Mortimer in a rich banking house. The possibilities of bold pilferings from the heaps of gold were most tempting to him, and he was now quite ready to commit himself to any feasible scheme to carry out Mortimer's evil design. The old fence was an unscrupulous man, and he was ready to go to almost any length in crime to avail himself of an opportunity so tempting to his greed of gain.

The two confederates discussed the matter for some time, and at length they agreed upon a plan of action, which boded ill for our hero.

CHAPTER VI.

A RAY OF SUNSHINE.

YOUNG Randolph entered upon his duties at once, but of course did little more during the day than familiarize himself with the work that had been assigned to him. Toward evening a ray of sunshine burst joyously into the bank, and threw a bright cheerful glow over the office.

Ray Goldwin, the light hearted, merry daughter of the senior partner, with her sunny face and winning manners, was like a clear June morning.

Little acts go far, many times, to make one happy or quite miserable. It so happened that our hero had been doing some writing for Mr. Goldwin's own personal use. It lay upon his desk and was admirably done. It was, in fact, like copper plate. The whole arrangement of the work was artistic and in the best of taste.

"Oh, papa, who did this beautiful writing for you?" said Ray, enthusiastically.

"Our new clerk, Mr. Randolph," responded her father, nodding his head in the direction of Herbert. The latter felt his cheeks grow rosy at this compliment.

"Mr. Randolph," continued the banker, "will you kindly help me take these parcels out to my carriage?"

"Certainly, sir, with pleasure," replied Herbert, politely.

YOUNG RANDOLPH HANDED RAY INTO THE CARRIAGE WITH JUST ENOUGH EMBARRASSMENT IN HIS MANNER TO INTEREST HER.

Ray Goldwin looked at him with surprise; and his handsome face and fine form attracted even more than a passing glance from her.

"I want to run up to the corner of Broadway," said Mr. Goldwin, when they had reached the door. "John, you may call for me," he continued, addressing the coachman; "I will be ready by the time you get there."

Young Randolph handed Ray into the carriage, with just enough embarrassment in his manner to interest her. Then he placed the parcels on the seat beside her, receiving meanwhile a smile and a look that fully rewarded him. Raising his hat, he turned away, and as the coachman drove off he made a hasty retreat for the bank, from which the sunshine now seemed to have departed.

When he started for home at the close of business hours, two figures stood on the opposite side of the street, a little nearer Broadway.

As Herbert opened the outer door, preparatory to passing out, he took a position that brought his eyes directly upon them. One of them, uneasily, but perhaps quite naturally, placed a hand on the shoulder of his companion, while with the other he pointed directly at Herbert. Then, as if realizing that possibly he had been detected in this act, he nervously pointed to something on the top of the building, and all the while talked rapidly. This was sufficient to arrest our hero's attention. He watched the two sharply for a few minutes while standing upon the steps of the banking house.

Under his direct gaze they appeared somewhat nervous, and finally moved off in the direction of Broadway. Herbert followed them, or rather followed out his purpose to go up to City Hall Park, and find, if possible, Bob Hunter. Before reaching

Broadway, however, the two young fellows who had pointed at him stopped and peered into a show window, thus bringing their backs full upon Herbert as he passed them.

He knew so little of city life that he was slow to form an opinion, thinking that what seemed odd and suspicious to him would perhaps be all right in New York. He therefore dismissed the matter from his mind, and watched with amazement the crowds of men who at that hour of the day were pouring up Broadway, on their way home from business.

"What a great city this is!" he thought; "and it is American, too. I wonder if any of the cities of the Old World can turn out such a lot of business men as these!"

The boy was right in asking himself this question. The wonder he felt was natural, for a finer body of men can rarely be found than the business men of New York. And now he joined the stream that flowed northward. The massive buildings, tall and stately, on either side of Broadway, captured his admiration, and he gazed upon them with open mouthed amazement.

Stone buildings with gigantic pillars and massive walls; buildings ten or a dozen stories high, and mighty spires raising their tops afar up in mid air—all these added to the country lad's wonder and astonishment. He passed by the Western Union building, the Evening Post building, and now paused in front of the Herald office to read the "headings" on the bulletin board.

After being thus engaged for a few moments, he turned suddenly around, and, to his surprise, saw the two young fellows who had attracted his attention on Wall Street. One of them had a look about him that seemed familiar, and yet he could not tell where he had seen him. His figure, his eyes, and the shape of his face were not unlike Felix Mortimer; and yet he looked older than the latter by two or three years, for he wore a small mustache and tiny side whiskers. Seeing these same fellows the second time, and noticing that they were apparently watching him, made Herbert feel a trifle uneasy. But he was not easily worried or frightened.

Bob Hunter was in, as on the previous night, and very glad he seemed at his friend's good success in getting so desirable a position. He listened to Herbert's story of the contest with much interest, and then added thoughtfully:

"It might be a good idea to look out for that feller that seemed to get down on you so. He probably knows you are a stranger in the city, and——"

"Do you think there is any danger?" interrupted Herbert.

"No, I can't say as there is; but he might think, if he could get you out of the way, he would get the place with the banker. You said he was disappointed."

"Yes, he showed his disappointment very much."

"Well, nothing may come of it. You keep your eye on me, and I'll steer you through all right, I reckon."

Herbert was upon the point of telling Bob his suspicions about the two fellows that seemed to be shadowing him, and then it occurred to him that he might magnify the matter, and work himself into a state of uneasiness when it would be better to give it no thought whatever. Therefore he said nothing to the newsboy about them.

When they had finished dinner a little later, Bob asked him if he could manage to pass away an hour or so alone.

"Certainly, if you have an engagement," replied Herbert.

"I go to an evening school; but if you'll be lonesome

alone, why, I'll stay with you till you learn a thing or two about the city."

"Oh, I shall be all right," said our hero, confidently. "Don't think of remaining away from school on my account. I can enjoy looking at the sights here in the Bowery for a while; then I will go to the room, and read till you come."

"All right. I'll do as you say; but now you look out, Vermont, and don't get lost."

Bob seemed to have a fondness for calling his friend by this name, and the latter indulged him in the peculiarity without objection.

After a while, young Randolph drifted up to one of the Bowery dime museums, and stood there for some time reading the announcements, looking at the pictures, and watching the crowd that ebbed and flowed up and down that thoroughfare.

Presently a young fellow of about his own age, who had for some time been standing near him, made a casual remark about a comical looking person who had just passed by. Our hero looked up, and seeing that the remark had been addressed to him, he replied promptly. A conversation between him and the stranger followed. Herein Herbert showed the trustfulness characteristic of a country boy. He knew he was honest himself, and did not once suspect that the agreeable young man was playing the confidence game upon him.

CHAPTER VII.

BOB HUNTER THOROUGHLY AROUSED.

WHEN Bob Hunter returned from the evening school to his room, he expected to find young Randolph there.

"He promised to be here," said Bob to himself; "I hope nothing has happened to him."

The newsboy's manner showed some alarm. He felt anxious about his friend.

"Something has gone wrong, I believe, or he would surely come," continued Bob, after waiting for a full half hour; "but I can't imagine what has steered him on to the wrong track."

Another half hour went by, and Herbert did not put in an appearance.

"I might's well stay here, I s'pose, as to go 'n' prowl round this town huntin' for Vermont," said Bob, thoughtfully. "But I guess I'll see if I can strike his trail. Any way I'll feel better, 'cause I'll know I've done something. It's no use to let a feller like him be run into these dens, if the game can be stopped."

An hour's fruitless hunt, in and about the Bowery, failed to reveal Herbert's whereabouts to the anxious searcher. He was unable to find any one who remembered to have seen him.

After giving up all hope of learning what he wished to find out, Bob hurried back to his room, with a feeling of anxiety quite new to him. He had taken a great liking to our hero, and now felt thoroughly alarmed, fearing that foul play had been brought to bear upon him.

The next morning he was up bright and early, looking sharply after his paper business, but he was not the Bob Hunter of the past. From the drollest and funniest boy in the trade he had suddenly become the most serious and thoughtful.

"What's hit you this mornin', Bob?" said Tom Flannery, a companion newsboy.

"Why do you ask that?" returned Bob.

"Why, you look like you'd had a fit o' sickness."

"You're 'bout right, for I don't feel much like myself, no how. I didn't get no sleep hardly at all, and I've worried myself thin—just see here," and he pulled the waistband of his trousers out till there was nearly enough unoccupied space in the body of them to put in another boy of his size.

He couldn't resist the opportunity for a joke, this comical lad, not even now. The trousers had been given to him by one of his customers, a man of good size. Bob had simply shortened up the legs, so naturally there was quite a quantity of superfluous cloth about his slim body.

"Gewhittaker!" exclaimed Tom, "I should think you have fell off! But say, Bob, what's gone bad? What's done it?" continued Tom, disposed to be serious.

"Well, you know the boy I told you about, what's chummin' with me?"

"Yes, the one I saw you with last night, I s'pose?"

"Yes, the same one. Well, he is lost."

"Lost!" repeated Tom, incredulously.

BOB HUNTER, ALONE IN HIS ROOM, WONDERS WHAT HAS BECOME OF HIS NEW FRIEND.

"Yes;" and Bob acquainted him with the facts of Herbert's disappearance. "Now, what do you think of it?" he asked.

"Looks bad," said young Flannery, gravely.

"So it does to me."

"Foul play," suggested Tom.

"That's what I think."

"Perhaps he has got tired of New York and has lit out."

"No, not much. Vermont ain't no such boy."

"Well, you know him best. Did he have any grip or anything?"

"Yes, he had a good suit and lots of other truck."

"And they're in the room now?"

"Yes."

"You're in luck, Bob. I'd like a chum as would slope and leave me a good suit."

"Well, I wouldn't. No more would you, Tom Flannery," said Bob, slightly indignant.

"I didn't mean nothin'," said Tom, apologizing for the offense which he saw he had given. "Of course, I wouldn't want nobody to slope and leave his truck with me."

"That's all right then, Tom," said Bob, forgivingly. "But now, what do you s'pose has become of him?"

"Well, it looks like he didn't go of his own free will, when he left everything behind him."

"Of course it does, and I know he didn't."

Bob related the story of Herbert's experience at the bank, on the morning when he secured the position.

"I don't like that duffer—what d'ye call him?"

"Felix Mortimer," repeated Bob. "I'm sure that's the name Herbert give me."

"Well, I'll bet that he's put up the job."

"I think so myself. You see he knew Randolph wasn't no city chap."

"That's so, and he knew he'd have the drop on him. But I don't just see, after all, how he could get away with him."

"Well, he might have run him into some den or other."

"And drugged him?"

"Well, perhaps so. There are piles of ways them fellers have of doin' such jobs."

"I know they're kinder slick about it sometimes. But, say, Bob," continued Tom, earnestly, "what do you propose to do about it? He may be a prisoner."

"So he may, and probably is, if he is alive."

"Why, Bob, they wouldn't kill him, would they?"

"No, I don't suppose so, not if they didn't have to."

"Why would they have to do that?" asked Tom, with his eyes bulging out with excitement.

"Well, sometimes folks has to do so—them hard tickets will do 'most anything. You see, if they start in to make way with a feller, and they are 'fraid he'll blow on 'em, and they can't make no other arrangement, why then they just fix him so he won't never blow on nobody."

"Bob, it's awful, ain't it?" said Tom, with a shudder.

"Yes, it is. There are a pile of tough gangs in this city that don't care what they do to a feller."

"What do you s'pose they've done with your chum?" asked young Flannery, returning to the subject.

"Well, that's just what I want to know," said Bob, seriously. "I am going to try to find out, too. There are tough dens in them cross streets running out of the Bowery."

"They won't do worse nor keep him a prisoner, will they, Bob?"

"Probably they won't, not 'less they think he will blow on 'em. You see they've got to look out for themselves."

"That's so, Bob, but why couldn't they send him off somewhere so he couldn't blow on 'em?"

"They might do that, too."

"But they would get him so far away he couldn't get back to New York never, I suppose?"

"Yes, that's the idea. They might run him off to sea, and put him on an island, or somethin' like that. I can't say just what they might do if they have their own way. But the idea is this, Tom Flannery, *we must stop 'em,*" said Bob, emphatically, "you and me. We've got to find out where he is, and rescue him."

"That's the boss idea, Bob," replied Tom, with emphasis. "But I don't see just how we're goin' to do it, do you?"

"Well, no, I can't see the whole game, not now. But we must commence, and when we get a few points, we can slide ahead faster."

"I wouldn't know how to commence."

"Well, I do; I thought that all out last night, and I'm only waiting till ten o'clock. Then I'll steer for the bank where Herbert worked."

"Bob, you beat all the boys I know of," said Tom, eying him with admiration. "None of 'em would ever think of doin' the things you do, and they couldn't do 'em if they did, that's all. And now you're goin' to do the detective act!"

Tom stopped short here with a jerk, as if he had got to the end of his rope, and took a long breath. To "do the detective act" seemed to him the greatest possible triumph for a boy like himself. He looked upon his companion, therefore, with wonder and admiration.

TOM FLANNERY.

Bob's plans for penetrating the mystery had, indeed, been carefully formed. He fearlessly undertook an enterprise from which most boys would have shrunk. This keen, bright street lad, however, was not of the shrinking kind. He did not turn away from encountering dangers, even the dangers of some dreadful den in which he feared our hero was now a prisoner.

During the forenoon he visited the banking house of Richard Goldwin and there found Felix Mortimer already installed in Herbert's place. This discovery confirmed his worst fears and intensified his alarm for the safety of his friend.

CHAPTER VIII.

FELIX MORTIMER AT THE BANK.

"CAN I see the proprietor?" said a boy addressing a clerk at the counter of Richard Goldwin's bank. It was the morning after Herbert's mysterious disappearance.

"What is your name?" asked the clerk.

"Felix Mortimer," answered the boy.

"Mr. Goldwin is very busy," replied the man at the counter.

"Very well, I will wait," said Felix; and he seated himself in a chair in the outer office.

In a little while Mr. Goldwin came out of his private room, and, seeing young Mortimer there, recognized him.

"Good morning, young man," said he, kindly.

"Good morning," returned Felix, deferentially.

"Have you come to tell us what has become of young Randolph?" asked the banker.

"I don't understand you," said Felix, innocently. "I came because you asked me to do so."

"Yes, yes, I remember; but I referred to the disappearance of the boy I engaged at the time you applied for the position."

"Why, isn't he here?" asked Mortimer, feigning surprise.

"No, he hasn't been here today."

"What do you imagine is the trouble?"

"I do not know, unless, like so many other boys, he has got tired of the work, and has left it for some other position."

"That may be, and now you speak of it, I remember he said, the morning we were all waiting to see you, that if he failed to get this place he had another position in view that he could get, and that it would pay him five dollars a week."

Young Mortimer told this falsehood with the ease of a veteran. His manner could not have been more impressive had he been telling the truth.

"Five dollars a week!" exclaimed Mr. Goldwin. "And he came here for three. I don't see what his motive was."

"Perhaps he had a motive," suggested Mortimer.

"I don't understand you," replied the banker.

Felix shrugged his shoulders.

"What do you mean? Do you know anything about him?" pursued Mr. Goldwin, his suspicions aroused.

"No, sir—er—not much."

"Speak up, young man. Tell me what you know about this young Vermonter."

"Vermonter?" repeated Felix, with a rising inflection; and he smiled suggestively.

"Yes, Vermonter. Do you know anything to the contrary?"

"You know I was an applicant for this position, Mr. Goldwin, so I do not like to answer your question. I hope you will excuse me."

"I appreciate your sense of honor, young man," said Mr. Goldwin; "but it is to my interest to know the facts. If there is anything against him, I should be informed of it. Tell me what you know, and you will lose nothing by doing so."

With apparent reluctance, Felix yielded to the persuasion, and said:

"I was on Broadway with a friend of mine, at the close of business hours, the day that you hired this young fellow. We were walking along by the Herald building when he came up Broadway and stopped to read the news on the *Telegram* bulletin board. I said to my friend, with surprise, 'There is the fellow I told you about—the one that beat me this morning in getting the position at Goldwin's.' He looked at me incredulously and said: 'Why, you told me he was a country boy—from Vermont.'

"'So he is,' I replied. 'Stuff,' said he. 'I know him well. That was a clever dodge to play the country act.' I protested, but he convinced me that he was right. He is in a lawyer's office, so he has to be in court more or less, and he said he saw him up before Judge Duffy only a few days ago, charged with stealing a pocket book. The suspicion was strong against him, but there wasn't proof enough to fix the theft upon him. The Court came near sending him to the Island, though, for he had been arrested twice before, so my friend said."

"The young villain!" said the banker, when Felix had finished this black falsehood, which he told so glibly, and with such seeming reluctance, that Mr. Goldwin accepted it as all truth. "I am sorry I ever took him into my office," he continued. "I must have the bank carefully looked over, to see if he misappropriated anything, as he very likely did."

Felix said nothing, but seemed to look sorry for Herbert.

"Well," said Mr. Goldwin, after a pause, "is it too late to get you?"

"I don't know," answered Mortimer, hesitatingly. "I

would like to work for you, but would not feel right to take the position away from this Vermonter."

Felix laid a special stress upon the word "Vermonter."

"Take it away from him!" replied the banker, scornfully. "He cannot enter this bank again."

"But you see I would feel that I am the means of keeping him out of the position. You wouldn't have known about his deception if I hadn't told you."

Felix now used the word "deception" flippantly, and with no further apparent apology for applying it to our hero.

"That is all right," replied Mr. Goldwin; "I am glad to see you sensitive about injuring another. It is much to your credit that you feel as you do about it."

"Thank you," was the modest reply. "Then if you think it would look right, and you really want me, I will take the position."

"Of course we can get hundreds and thousands of boys, but I have taken a liking to you. When can you commence?"

"I can commence this morning, if you wish me to," said Felix.

"Very well, I wish you would—er, that is if you feel able. I notice your face is swollen, and perhaps you are not feeling well."

"Oh, that will not bother me," replied Mortimer, coolly. "I had a tooth filled yesterday, and have got cold in my jaw."

"You must suffer with it. It is swollen badly and looks red and angry," said the banker sympathetically.

"It does hurt a good deal, but will not trouble me about my work."

"It looks as if the skin had been injured—more like a

bruise, as if you had received a heavy blow on your jaw," said Mr. Goldwin, examining the swelling more closely.

Felix colored perceptibly, but immediately rallied, and said the poulticing had given it that appearance.

Could Mr. Goldwin have known the truth about this injured jaw, he would have been paralyzed at the bold falsehood of the young villain before him.

He had succeeded admirably in blackening our young hero's reputation. Mr. Goldwin now looked upon Herbert with ill favor, and even disgust. And this change was all caused by the cunning and falsehoods of young Mortimer. He had poisoned Mr. Goldwin's mind, and thus succeeded in establishing himself in the banker's good opinion and securing the coveted position.

"Another boy wants to see you, Mr. Goldwin," said the clerk, shortly after the man of finance had engaged young Mortimer.

"You may show him in," said the banker.

The door opened, and Bob Hunter stepped into Mr. Goldwin's presence. If he had only had a bundle of newspapers under his arm, he would have felt quite at home; but, as he had nothing of the kind, he was a trifle embarrassed.

"What do you want here?" asked Mr. Goldwin, more sharply than was his wont.

"I come down, sir, to see if you can tell me anything about Herbert Randolph."

"What do you want to know about him?"

"I want to know where he is. He hain't shown up not sence last night."

"Was he a friend of yours?"

"Yes, sir, me and him roomed together."

"You and he roomed together?" repeated the banker, as if he doubted Bob's word.

"That's what I said, sir," answered the newsboy, showing his dislike of the insinuation against his truthfulness.

"I am afraid you are inclined to be stuffy, young man," replied Mr. Goldwin. "I am unable, however, to give you the information you seek."

"You don't know where he is, then?"

"No, I have not seen him since he left here last night."

"Do you know why he is stayin' away?"

"Certainly I do not."

"Done nothin' wrong, I s'pose?" queried Bob.

"I have not fixed any wrong upon him yet."

"Then, if he hain't done no wrong, somethin's keepin' him."

"He may have a motive in staying away," said the banker, becoming interested in Bob's keen manner.

"What do you s'pose his motive is?"

"That I cannot tell."

"Foul play, that's what I think."

"Nonsense, boy."

"I don't think there's no nonsense about it. I know he wouldn't light out jest for fun, not much. Herbert Randolph wasn't no such a feller. He didn't have no money, 'n' he had to work. Me an' him had a room together, as I said, an' his things are in the room now."

"When did you see him last?" said Mr. Goldwin.

Bob explained all about Herbert's disappearance, but was careful to say nothing about his suspicions pointing to Felix Mortimer. He saw the latter in the outer office as he entered, and he thought policy bade him keep his suspicions to himself for the present.

"You tell a straightforward story, my boy," said Mr. Goldwin, "but I cannot think there has been any foul play. In fact, I have heard something against this young Randolph that makes me distrust him. Were it not for this, I should feel more interest in your story, and would do all in my power to try and find him."

BOB HUNTER SPEAKS UP FOR HERBERT.

"I don't believe there's nothing against him. He's an honest boy, if I know one when I see him. He liked you and his work, and them that speaks against him is dishonest themselves. That's what I think about it."

"But that is only your opinion. Certainly he does not appear in a favorable light at the present time."

Presently Bob departed from the bank. He had learned all he expected, and even more. He knew now that Felix Mortimer was in Herbert's place, that Mr. Goldwin had been influenced against his friend by what he believed to be falsehoods, and that Herbert's whereabouts was as much a mystery at the bank as to himself.

These facts pointed suspiciously to Felix Mortimer. Who else could want to get Herbert out of the way? Bob argued. Having thus settled the matter in his own mind, he was ready to commence testing his theories.

"Tom Flannery," said Bob, when he had returned from Wall Street, "I've struck the trail."

"No, you hain't, Bob, not so quick as this?" said Tom, with surprise.

Bob explained what he had learned at the bank.

"Now," said he, "I want you, Tom, to look out for my business tonight. Get some kid to help you, and mind you see he does his work right."

"What you goin' to do, Bob?"

"I'm going to lay round Wall Street till that Mortimer feller comes outer the bank."

"What do you mean? You hain't goin' to knock him out, are you, Bob?"

"Shucks, Tom, you wouldn't make no kind of a detective. Of course I wouldn't do that. Why, that would spoil the whole game."

"Well, then, what are you goin' to do?"

"Why, I'll do just as any detective would—follow him, of course."

"Is that the way they do it, Bob?"

"Some of 'em do, when they have a case like this one."

"This is a gosh fired hard one, ain't it, Bob?"

"Well, 'tain't no boy's play—not a case like this one."

"So you're goin' to foller him? I wish I could go with you, Bob."

"But, you see, you must sell papers. I'll want you to help me later, when I get the case well worked up."

"It'll be too big for one detective then, I s'pose?"

"That's the idea, Tom. Then I'll call you in," said Bob, with the swell of a professional.

"I wish 'twas all worked up, Bob, so you'd want to call me in now, as you call it. It'll be exciting, won't it?"

"Well, I should think it would, before we get through with it."

"Say, Bob, will there be any fightin'?" asked Tom, eagerly. He was already excited over the prospects.

"Can't say that now—hain't got the case worked up enough to tell. 'Tain't professional to say too much about a case. None of the detectives does it, and why should I? That's what I want to know, Tom Flannery."

"Well, you shouldn't, Bob, if the rest doesn't do it."

"Of course not. It's no use to be a detective, unless the job is done right and professional. I believe in throwin' some style into anything like this. 'Tain't often, you know, Tom, when a feller gets a real genuine case like this one. Why, plenty er boys might make believe they had cases, but they'd be baby cases—only baby cases, Tom Flannery, when you'd compare 'em with this one—a real professional case."

"I don't blame you for bein' proud, Bob," said Tom, admiringly. "I only wish I had such a case."

"Why, you've got it now; you're on it with me, hain't you? Don't you be silly now, Tom. You'll get all you want before you get through with this case; an', when it's all published in the papers, your name will be printed with mine."

"Gewhittaker!" exclaimed Tom; "I didn't think of that before. Will our names really be printed, Bob?"

"Why, of course they will. Detectives' names are always printed, hain't they? You make me tired, Tom Flannery. I should think you'd know better. Don't make yourself so redickerlous by askin' any more questions like that. But just you tend to business, and you'll get all the glory you want—professional glory, too."

"It'll beat jumpin' off the Brooklyn Bridge, won't it?" said Tom.

"Well, if you ain't an idiot, Tom Flannery, I never saw one. To think of comparin' a detective with some fool that wants cheap notoriety like that! You just wait till you see your name in big letters in the papers along with mine. It'll be Bob Hunter and Tom Flannery."

Tom's eyes bulged out with pride at the prospect. He had never before realized so fully his own importance.

CHAPTER IX.

BOB ASSUMES A DISGUISE.

AT the close of business hours, Felix Mortimer sauntered up Broadway with something of an air of triumph about him. His jaw was still swollen, and doubtless pained him not a little.

Another boy passed up Broadway at the same time, and only a little way behind Mortimer.

It was Bob Hunter, and he managed to keep the same distance between himself and young Mortimer, whom, in fact, he was "shadowing." Of course, Mortimer knew nothing of this. In fact, he did not know such a boy as Bob Hunter existed.

At the post office Felix Mortimer turned into Park Row. He stopped and read the bulletins at the *Mail and Express* office. Then he bought an evening paper, and, standing on the steps of the *World* office, looked it over hastily.

Now he moved on up Publishers' Row, passing the *Times*, the *Tribune*, and the *Sun* buildings, and walked along Chatham Street. Presently he emerged into the Bowery. Now he walked more rapidly than he had been doing, so that Bob had to quicken his pace to keep him in sight.

At the corner of Pell Street and the Bowery he met a young man who seemed to be waiting for him.

"I've been hanging round here for 'most half an hour," said he, as if displeased.

"I'm here on time," replied Felix; "just half past five. Come, let's have a glass of beer."

Peter Smartweed was the name of this young fellow, as Bob afterwards found out.

When Felix and his friend passed into the drinking saloon, Bob followed them as far as the door; then he turned back, and sought the disguise of a bootblack.

A young knight of the brush stood near by, with his blacking box slung over his shoulder. Bob arranged with him for the use of it for a few moments, promising to pay over to him all the proceeds he made thereby. He also exchanged his own hat for the cap the boy had on, and, with this head gear pulled down over the left side of his face, the appearance of Bob Hunter was much changed. His accustomed step, quick, firm, and expressive, was changed to that of the nerveless, aimless boy—a sort of shuffle.

Thus disguised, he approached Felix Mortimer and his companion, who were sitting at a table with a partially filled schooner of beer before each of them.

"Shine? shine, boss?" said Bob, in a strange voice.

No response was made by the convivial youths.

"Two for five!" continued Bob, persistently. "Two reg'lar patent leathers for only five cents!"

Peter looked at his boots. They were muddy. Then he argued with himself that Felix had paid for the beer, so it seemed to him that he could not even up the score in any less expensive way than by paying for the shines.

"Do you mean you will give us both a shine for five cents?" said Peter.

"Yes," drawled Bob, lazily.

"Well, see that they are good ones, now, or I'll not pay you a cent."

Bob commenced work on the shoes very leisurely. He seemed the embodiment of stupidity, and blundered along in every way possible to prolong the time.

"How would you like to climb down, Mort, and shine shoes for a living?" said Peter Smartweed, jokingly.

"Perhaps I wouldn't mind it if I was stupid as the kid fumbling around your shoes seems to be," replied Felix, in a more serious mood than his companion.

"Well, I think you looked even more stupid than this young Arab last night, when you lay upon the floor."

BOB HUNTER PLAYS THE DETECTIVE.

"Well, I guess you would have felt stupid, too, if you had got such a clip as I did," retorted Felix, as he nursed his swollen jaw with his hand.

"It was a stunning blow, for a fact. John L. Sullivan couldn't have done it neater. I didn't think, Mort, that that young countryman could hit such a clip, did you?"

"No, I didn't; and I'm mighty sure you don't realize now what a stinging blow he hit me. You talk about it as if it didn't amount to much. Well, all I've got to say is, I don't want to see you mauled so, but I wish you knew how good it felt to be floored the way I was."

"No, thank you," said Peter; "I don't want any of it. But you looked so comical, as you fell sprawling, that I couldn't help laughing. I believe I would have laughed if you had been killed."

Bob Hunter's ears were now wide open.

"I couldn't see anything to laugh about," said Felix, bitterly.

"That isn't very strange, either. You naturally wouldn't, under the circumstances," laughed young Smartweed.

"Come, now, let up," said Felix. "Your turn may come."

"I expect it will, if this young farmer ever gets after me."

"But you don't expect him to get out, do you?"

"I hadn't thought much about it. My part of the programme was to get him into old Gunwagner's den, and I did it without any accident."

Felix looked hard at his companion. He knew the last part of this sentence was a sarcastic thrust at him.

Bob grew excited, and found it difficult to restrain himself. He felt certain now that these two young villains were talking about his friend Herbert Randolph.

"No accident would have happened to me, either, if he hadn't hit me unawares," protested young Mortimer, with a bit of sourness about his manner. "I allow I could get away with him in a fair fight."

"Oh, no, you couldn't, Mort; he is too much for you. I could see that in a minute, by the way he handled himself."

Young Mortimer's face flushed. He didn't like the comparison.

"Well, he won't bother me again very soon," said he, vindictively.

"Didn't they tumble to anything crooked at the bank?" asked Peter, after a few moments' serious thought.

"No."

"I don't see why. The circumstances look suspicious."

"Well, they didn't suspect the truth."

"You're in luck, then, that is all I have to say."

"I shall be, you mean, when we get him out of the way."

"He seems to be pretty well out of your way now."

"But that won't last forever. He must be got out of New York, that's all. Old Gunwagner will not keep him round very long, you may be sure of that."

"You don't know how to shine a shoe," growled Smartweed to our young detective. "See the blacking you have put on the upper! Wipe it off, I say; at once, too."

Bob's blood boiled with indignation, and he was about to reply sharply, when he remembered that he was now acting the detective, and so he said:

"All right, boss; I'll fix it fer yer;" and he removed the superfluous blacking with great care. There was no longer any doubt in his mind about Herbert being a prisoner. He was satisfied that his friend was in the clutches of old Gunwagner, and he knew from the conversation that he was in danger of being lost forever to New York and to his friends.

The situation was an alarming one. Bob pictured vividly the worst possibilities of our hero's fate.

Presently, after young Smartweed had lighted a cigarette and taken a few puffs, he said, absentmindedly:

"So you are going to send him away from New York?"

"Of course, you don't s'pose we would be very safe with him here, do you?" replied Mortimer.

"Safe enough, so long as he is in old Gunwagner's cell. But what is to be done with him? Send him back to Vermont?"

"Not much; he won't go there unless he escapes."

"It's rough on the fellow, Mort, to run him off to sea, or to make him a prisoner in the bottom of a coal barge or canal boat. But that is what he is likely to get from that old shark," said Peter Smartweed, meaning Gunwagner.

"Don't you get soft hearted now," replied Felix, in a hard voice.

"I'm not soft hearted, Mort, and you know it, but I don't like this business, any way."

"What did you go into it for, then?"

"What do we do anything for? I thought, from what you said, that he was a coarse young countryman. But he don't seem like it. In fact I believe he is too nice a fellow to be ruined for life."

"Perhaps you'd better get him out then," said Mortimer, sarcastically.

"You talk like a fool," replied Smartweed, testily.

"So do you," retorted his companion, firing up; and he nursed his aching jaw as if to lend emphasis to his remarks. These explosions suddenly ended the discussion, and as soon as their shoes were polished, the two young villains left the saloon. Mortimer turned up the Bowery, and Smartweed passed into a side street leading towards Broadway.

Bob readily dropped his assumed character of bootblack, and quickly started in pursuit of Felix Mortimer.

The latter went directly home, where he remained for nearly an hour. At the end of this time, he emerged from the house, much to the young detective's relief. He had waited outside all this time, patiently watching for Felix's reappearance.

Though cold and hungry, Bob could not afford to give up the chase long enough even to get a bit of lunch. He had made wonderful progress so far in his detective work, and he felt, as he had a right to feel, highly elated over his discoveries.

Now he was shadowing young Mortimer again. Down the Bowery they went till they came to a side street in a disreputable locality. Here they turned towards the East River, and presently Felix Mortimer left the sidewalk and disappeared within the door of an old building.

"So this is Gunwagner's, is it?" said Bob to himself. "At least I s'pose 'tis, from what them fellers said—Gunwagner—yes, that's the name. Well, this may not be it, but I'm pretty sure it is," he continued, reasoning over the problem.

After fixing the house and its locality securely in his mind, and after having waited till he satisfied himself that Mortimer intended remaining there for a time, he made a lively trip to City Hall Park, where he joined young Flannery.

"Well, Bob, have you struck anything?" said Tom, instantly, and with much more than a passing interest.

"Yes; I've struck it rich—reg'lar detective style, I tell you, Tom," said Bob, with pride and enthusiasm. And then he briefly related all his discoveries.

"Nobody could er worked the business like you, Bob," said Tom, admiringly.

"Well, I did throw a little style into it, I think myself," replied Bob. "But," he continued, "there's no time now for talking the matter over. We've got some work to do. I've got the place located, and I want you to go with me now, and see what we can do."

Within five minutes the two boys were on their way to Christopher Gunwagner's, and as they passed hurriedly along the streets they formed a hasty plan for immediate action—a plan cunningly devised for outwitting this miserable old fence and his villainous companions.

CHAPTER X.

SOMETHING ABOUT HERBERT RANDOLPH.

HAD our young hero been more wary, he would not have so easily fallen a victim to the deceit of the genial stranger whom he met on the Bowery. He should have been more cautious, and less ready to assume friendly relations with a stranger. His lack of prudence in this respect was almost inexcusable, inasmuch as he had been warned by Bob Hunter to look out for himself. Moreover, his suspicions should have been excited by the two young fellows he saw on Wall Street, who appeared to be shadowing him.

But none of these prudential thoughts seemed to occur to young Randolph. In Vermont, he spoke to every one with a frank, open confidence. He had always done so from his earliest recollections. Others in his locality did the same. Unrestrained social intercourse was the universal custom of the people. Habit is a great power in one's life. It guided our hero on this fatal night, and he talked freely and confidentially with his new acquaintance.

"Have you ever been in one of these Bowery museums?" asked the genial young man, after they had chatted for a little time.

"No, I have not," replied Herbert, in a hesitating manner that implied his desire to enter.

This young man was the same one whose boots Bob Hunter blackened when he was acting the detective, otherwise Peter Smartweed.

The latter smiled at the readiness with which young Randolph caught at the bait.

"Well, you have missed a treat," said he, with assumed surprise.

"I suppose so," replied Herbert, feeling that his education had been neglected.

"They have some wonderful curiosities in some of these museums," continued the young confidence scamp.

"So I should think, from the looks of these pictures."

"But this is the poorest museum on the Bowery. There are some great curiosities in some of them, and a regular show."

"Have you been in all of them?" asked Herbert.

"Oh, yes, dozens of times. Why, I can go into one of the museums whenever I like, without paying a cent, and it is the best one in New York."

"Can you?" said Herbert, with surprise. "I wish I could go in free."

"I can fix that for you all right," said Peter, magnanimously. "I often take a friend in with me."

"And it doesn't cost you anything?"

"No, not a cent. If you like, we will stroll down the Bowery, and drop in for a little while. By the way, I remember now that a new curiosity, a three headed woman, is on exhibition there."

"A three headed woman!" exclaimed Herbert; "she must be a wonderful sight!"

"So she is. Come on, let's go and see her. It is not down very far. You have nothing to do, I suppose?"

"No, only to pass the time away for an hour or so."

"Very well, then, you can't pass it in any more agreeable way than this, I am sure."

"You are very kind," replied Herbert, as they moved off in the direction of the supposed museum. He had no thought of danger, as he walked along with his new friend, happy in anticipation of the pleasure before him. Could he, however, have realized that he was the victim of a shrewd confidence game, that every step he now took was bringing him nearer to the trap that had been set for him by cruel, unscrupulous villains, how his whole being would have revolted against the presence of the unprincipled fellow beside him, who was now coolly leading him on to his ruin.

A SURPRISE FOR FELIX MORTIMER.

Presently they turned up a side street, and soon stopped before a low, ugly building.

"The museum is on the next street," remarked young Smartweed, as he rang the bell three times. "We have to walk through this court, to reach it by the back passage."

Still Herbert's suspicions slumbered.

And now the catch to the door was pulled back, and our unfortunate hero and his companion passed in. The hallway was ominously dark. They groped their way forward till a second door was reached, and here the leader knocked three times, then paused for a moment and knocked once more.

After a brief interval three more knocks precisely like the first were given, and then the door opened.

The two stepped quickly into the room, and Herbert's arms were instantly seized by some one from behind the door, and drawn backward by an effort to fasten the wrists together behind him. Quicker than thought, young Randolph wrested his arms from the grip that was upon them, and, turning like a flash, planted a solid blow upon the jaw of his assailant—a blow which sent him, with a terrified yell, sprawling to the floor.

Then it was that he recognized, in the prostrate figure, Felix Mortimer, and a sickening sense of the awful truth dawned upon him. He was trapped!

The genial friend whom he had met on the Bowery now showed his real character, and before Herbert could further defend himself, he was pounced upon by him and a villainous looking man with a scraggy red beard and most repulsive features. They threw a thick black cloth over his head, and, after binding his hands firmly together, thrust him into a dark vault, or pen, in the cellar.

Our hero realized now most fully his helpless and defenseless position—a position that placed him entirely at the mercy of his enemies; if mercy in any degree dwelt in the breasts of the cruel band of outlaws in whose den he was now a prisoner.

CHAPTER XI.

IMPRISONED AT THE FENCE.

"THIS is a fine beginning to a city career—short but brilliant," said young Randolph to himself, bitterly, as he mused upon his deplorable situation.

"Fool that I was! It's all plain enough to me now," he continued, after a half hour's deep thought, in which he traced back, step by step, his experiences since landing in the big city. "I ought to have recognized him at once—the villain! He is the very fellow I saw across the street with his pal, as I left the bank. I thought he looked familiar, but I've seen so many people in this great town that I'm not surprised at my miss. Mighty bad miss, though; one that has placed me in a box trap, and under ground at that."

Herbert was right in his conclusions. The fellow who had so cleverly played the confidence game upon him was the same one who awaited his appearance in Wall Street, and afterwards shadowed him up Broadway.

"This must all be the work of that young villain Mortimer," continued Herbert, still reasoning on the subject. "I ought to have been sharper; Bob told me to look out for him. If I had had any sense, I could have seen that he meant to be revenged upon me. I knew it, and yet I didn't want to admit, even to myself, that I was at all uneasy. He must have been the same one that pointed me out to this confidence fellow on Wall Street. He was probably made up with false side whiskers and mustache, so that I wouldn't recognize him.

"Well," said he, starting up suddenly from his reverie, "how is all this reasoning about how I came to get into this trap going to help me to get out of it? That is what I want to know;" and he commenced exploring his dark, damp cell, in search of some clew that would aid him in solving the problem.

He was not alarmed about his personal safety. Up to this time, happily, no such thought had entered his mind. He sanguinely looked upon his imprisonment as merely temporary.

In this opinion, however, he erred greatly. The same rural credulity that made him the victim of Peter Smartweed, now led him to suppose that the unscrupulous rascals who held him a prisoner would soon release him. He looked upon the matter as simply one of revenge on the part of Mortimer. He little realized his true situation, and did not even dream of the actual significance of his imprisonment. He therefore felt a sense of genuine consolation when he thought of the well deserved blow he had delivered upon his enemy's jaw; and several times, as he prowled around the cell, he laughed heartily, thinking of Mortimer's ridiculous appearance as he lay stretched upon the floor.

Herbert Randolph was full of human nature, and human nature of the best sort—warm blooded, natural, sensible. There was nothing pale and attenuated about him. He was full of spirits, was manly, kind and generous, and yet he could appreciate heartily a point honorably gained on the enemy. Thus instead of giving himself up to despair and grief, he tried to derive all the comfort possible out of his situation.

His cell was dark as night. He could not see his own hands, and the dampness and musty odor, often noticeable in old cellars, added much to his discomfort. He found that the cell was made of strong three inch slats, securely bolted to thick timbers. These strips, or slats, were about three inches apart. The door was made in the same manner, and was fastened with a padlock. Altogether his cell was more like a cage than anything else; however, it seemed designed to hold him securely against all efforts to escape from his captors.

The door, as previously stated, was fastened by a padlock. Herbert learned this by putting his hands through the slats, and carefully going over every part of the fastening arrangement.

This discovery gave him slight hopes. The lock he judged to be one of the ordinary cheap ones such as his father always used on his cornhouse and barn doors. Now he had on several occasions opened these locks by means of a stiff wire, properly bent. Therefore, should this lock prove to be one of the same kind, and should fortune place within his reach a suitable piece of wire, or even a nail of the right sort, he felt that he could make good his escape from this cell.

"But should I succeed in this," he very prudently reasoned, "would I be any better off? That heavy trap door is undoubtedly fastened down, and, so far as I know, that is the only means of exit; but—— What is that?" he suddenly said to himself, as he felt the cold shivers creep over him.

The sound continues. It seems like rasping or grating. Louder and more distinct it grows, as Herbert's imagination becomes more active.

Every sound to one in his situation, in that dark, lonesome

cellar, could easily be interpreted to mean many forms of danger to him. But at length he reasons, from the irregular rasping, and from other slight evidences, that this noise is the gnawing of hungry rats.

What a frightful and alarming discovery this is to him! It strikes terror to his brave young heart, and makes cold beads of perspiration stand out upon his brow. And as these silent drops—the evidence of suffering—trickle down his face one by one, chilly and dispiriting, he grows sick to the very core.

Alone in a dark, damp cellar, with no means of defense—not even a stick, a knife, or any sort of implement to protect himself from the hordes of rats that now surround him.

This indeed is a night of terror to our young hero. He does not dare to throw himself upon the bench, lest he should sleep, and, sleeping, be attacked by these dreadful rats.

Accordingly, he commenced walking back and forth in his cell, as a caged tiger walks hour after hour from one end to the other of his narrow confines.

"This will keep me awake," said he to himself, with an attempt to rouse his spirits; "and it will also keep the rats away."

After he had paced thus for a time, he heard steps above him, and instantly he called out for aid. He called again and again, but the inhuman ear of old Gunwagner was deaf to his imploring cries.

The sound of footsteps was soon lost, and all was still save the gnawing of the rats. Herbert listened quietly for a time, to study their movements. Soon he heard them scampering about in all parts of the cellar. From the noise they made he judged them to be very large; and they were certainly bold, for now they were running about in contemptuous disregard of young Randolph's presence. Occasionally he would yell at them, and kick vigorously upon the framework of his cell. By this means he kept them at a somewhat respectful distance.

And now his mind reverted again to the cause of his imprisonment. As the long, weary hours dragged by, he studied the matter with the utmost care, giving painstaking thought tó the slightest details and the most trivial acts. His points were, consequently, well made. They were reasonable, logical, probable. The scheme broadened as he progressed. What he had supposed to be a mere matter of revenge now loomed up clearly and distinctly before him as a bold plot against himself—a piece of outrageous villainy that fairly appalled him.

He saw Felix Mortimer in his place in the bank; saw himself looked upon by Mr. Goldwin with suspicion and disgust. And this feeling, he knew, would extend to his daughter—bright, winsome Ray.

It was odd that Herbert should think of her in this connection, while in such mental agony. He had seen her but once, and then only for a minute. True, she was wonderfully pretty, and her manner was irresistibly attractive, but young Randolph was of a serious turn of mind. No, he was not one to become infatuated with any girl, however charming; he never had been, and, to use his own language, he did not propose to become so. But he could not help thinking of Ray in connection with this matter. He recalled how her sunny presence lighted up the bank that very afternoon, and in imagination he saw her bright, mischievous blue eyes, brimful of fun and merriment, as he handed her into her carriage.

"She did look sweet, confounded if she didn't," said Herbert to himself, forgetting for the time his sorrow; "sweet and pretty as a peach, and her cheeks had the same rich, delicate tint. Her hair—— Great Scott!" ejaculated young Randolph, suddenly awaking to what he had been saying. "Another evidence of my being a fool. I'd better have stayed on the farm," he continued, more or less severely.

"Well, I'm a prisoner," he said, sadly, after a thoughtful

YOUNG RANDOLPH AT LAST FALLS ASLEEP EXHAUSTED.

pause. "It doesn't matter much what I think or say. But, somehow or other, I wish I had never seen her," he continued, meditatively. "Now she will think of me only with contempt, just as her father will. Of course she will; it would be only natural."

Exhausted, weary, and even overburdened with oppressive thought, he sat down on the wooden bench in his cell. The rats still gnawed and frolicked, and prowled at will. Herbert listened to them for a moment; then he thought of his dear mother and father, of his home, his own comfortable bed.

A stray tear now stole down his cheeks, and then another. The poor boy was overcome, and he gave way to a sudden outburst of grief. Then he rested his head in his hand, and tried to think again. But his mind was wearied to exhaustion.

"My mother, my mother and father! Oh, how I wish I could see them! What would they do if they only knew where I am?"

He paused after this utterance; and now his thoughts suddenly ceased their weary wanderings. All was quiet, and the long measured breathing gave evidence that our young hero slept.

CHAPTER XII.

BOB'S BRILLIANT MOVE.

"BUT I say, Bob, I don't jest see how we are goin' to get into that den," said Tom Flannery, thoughtfully, as he and his companion hurried along towards old Gunwagner's.

"Don't you?" replied Bob, carelessly, as if the matter was of trivial importance.

"No, I don't. Do you, Bob?"

"Do you think, Tom Flannery, that a detective is goin' to tell all he knows—is goin' to give away the game before it's played?" said Bob, with feigned displeasure.

He asked this question to evade the one put to him.

"I thought they always told them as was in the secret, don't they?"

"Well, I must say you have some of the ignorantest ideas of any boy I ever see," said Bob, with assumed surprise.

Young Flannery looked sad, and made no reply.

"The trouble with you, Tom, is that you worry too much," continued the juvenile detective.

"I ain't worryin', Bob. What made you think that? I only wanted to know what's the racket, an' what I've got to do."

"Well, you s'pose I bro't you up here to do somethin', don't you?"

"Of course you did, Bob. But what is it? That's what I want to know."

"You ask more questions than any feller I ever see, Tom Flannery. Now you jest tell me what any detective would do, on a case like this one is, and tell me what he'd want you to do, an' then I'll tell you what I want you to do."

Tom looked grave, and tried hard to think.

The fact of the matter is that Bob himself hardly knew what step to take next, in order to carry out the plan he had formed. But his reputation was at stake. He thought he must make a good showing before Tom, though the matter of gaining an entrance to Gunwagner's was far from clear to him. He therefore wanted Tom's opinion, but it would not do to ask him for it, so he adopted this rather sharp device.

"Blamed if I can tell, Bob, what a detective would do," replied Tom. "You see I ain't no natural detective like you. But I should think he'd swoop down on the den and scoop it."

"And that's what you think a reg'lar detective would do?"

"Yes. I don't see nothin' else for him to do."

"Well, how would he do it?"

"I ain't no detective, Bob, so I don't know."

"I didn't s'pose you did know, Tom Flannery, so now I'll tell you," said Bob, who had seized upon his companion's suggestion. "A regular detective, if he was in my place, and had you to help him, would do jest what I'm going to do, and that is to send you into the den first, to see what you can find out."

"Send me in?" exclaimed Tom, incredulously.

"Yes, that's what I said, wasn't it?"

"And that's what a reg'lar detective would do?"

"Yes."

"And that's what you're goin' to do?"

"Yes, of course it is. Why wouldn't I do the same as any other detective? That's what I want to know."

"Of course you would, Bob, but I couldn't do nothin' if I should go in," said Tom, gently protesting against the proposed plan of action.

"You can do what I tell you to, can't you?"

"I don't know nothin' about it, any way, I tell you," replied Tom, showing more plainly his disinclination to obedience.

"Tom Flannery, I wouldn't er believed that you would back out this way," said Bob, with surprise.

"Well, I don't want to be a detective no way. I don't care nothin' about my name bein' in the paper."

"You hain't got no ambition. If you had, you'd show some spunk now. 'Tain't often a feller has a chance to get into a case like this one is."

"Well, I don't care if it ain't, that's what I say."

"I thought you wanted to be a detective, and couldn't wait, hardly, for me to work up the case."

"Well, I didn't think I'd have to climb into places like this old Gunwagner's. 'Tain't what I call bein' a detective no way."

"You make me tired, Tom Flannery. You get the foolishest notions into your head of any boy I ever see."

"Well, I don't care if I do. I know plenty detectives don't do nothin' like this. They jest dress up and play the gentleman, that's what they do."

"And that's the kind of a detective you want to be, is it?"

"Yes, it is; there ain't no danger about that kind of bein' a detective."

"Tom, you'd look great tryin' to be a gentleman, wouldn't you? I'd like to see you, Tom Flannery, a gentleman!" said Bob, derisively. "It makes me sick, such talk."

Tom was silent for a time. Evidently he thought there was some ground for Bob's remarks.

But an idea occurred to him now.

"Bob," said he, "if you like bein' this kind of a detective, why don't you go in yourself, instead of sendin' me? Now, answer me that, will you?"

"It wouldn't be reg'lar professional like, and then there wouldn't be no style about it."

Tom made no reply. In fact there seemed nothing further for him to say; Bob's answer left no chance for argument.

The two boys now stood opposite Gunwagner's. Presently a boy with a package in his hand approached the house, and, looking nervously about him, as if he feared he was watched, walked up the stoop and rang the bell three times. He did not see the two young detectives, as they were partially hidden by a big telegraph pole.

After a time the door opened, and he passed in. Bob noticed that it was very dark inside, and wondered why no light shone.

"I couldn't get in, nohow, if I wanted to," said Tom, trying to justify himself for his seeming cowardice.

"Does look so," assented Bob, absent mindedly.

"I wouldn't like to be a prisoner in there; would you, Bob?"

"No, of course I wouldn't."

"I wish we could get your chum out."

"I wish so, too; but you don't s'pose we can do it by standing here, do you?"

"No, but I don't know nothin' to do; do you, Bob?"

"If I told you what to do, you wouldn't do it."

"Well, I didn't see no sense in my goin' in there alone, nohow."

"I did, if you didn't. I wanted you to look round and see what you could find out, and post me, so when I went in I could do the grand act."

"I wouldn't a' got out to post you, Bob. They'd a' kept me—that's what they'd done."

The door now opened, and out came the same boy who but a few minutes before had entered the Gunwagner den. He looked cautiously about him, and then started down the street toward the East River. He was a small boy, of about twelve years of age, while our two detectives were several years his senior. From remarks dropped by Felix Mortimer and Peter Smartweed, Bob surmised that Gunwagner might keep a fence, and the suspicious manner of this small boy confirmed his belief.

"Here's our chance," whispered Bob, nervously. "You follow this boy up, and don't let him get away from you. I'll rush ahead and cut him off. Keep close to him, so we can corner him when I whistle three times."

"All right," said Tom, with his old show of enthusiasm, and each commenced the pursuit.

Between Allen and Orchard Streets the detectives closed in on the small boy. Bob had put himself fairly in front of him, and Tom followed close behind. The chief detective slackened his pace very perceptibly, and seemed to be trying to make out the number on the house before which he now halted.

"Can you tell me where old Gunwagner lives?" said he, addressing the small boy, who was now about to pass by.

The boy stopped suddenly, and the color as suddenly left his face.

Bob had purposely chosen this locality, close to a gaslight, so that he might note the effect of his question upon the boy. Now he gave the signal as agreed upon, and Tom instantly came up and took a position that made retreat for the lad impossible. The latter saw this, and burst into tears. Conscious of his own guilt, he needed no further accuser to condemn him.

"Don't take it so hard," said Bob; "you do the square thing, and we won't blow on you—will we, Tom?"

"No, we won't," replied the latter.

"We saw you when you went into Gunwagner's—saw the package in your hand, and know the whole game," continued Bob. "Now, if you will help us put up a job, why, we will let you off; but if you don't come down square and do the right thing, why, we will jest run you in, and you'll get a couple of years or more on the Island. Now what do you say?"

"What do you want me to do?" sobbed the small boy, trembling with fear.

"I want you to go back with us, and take me into Gunwagner's."

Tom was an interested listener, for he knew nothing about Bob's plans or purposes.

From further questionings, and many threats, our detectives found that a number of boys were in the habit of taking stolen goods to this miserable old fence. The number mixed up in the affair Bob did not learn, but he ascertained the fact that Felix Mortimer had often been seen there by this lad.

"Now me and Tom are doin' the detective business," said the chief; "and if you want to be a detective with us, you can join right in."

"I want to go home," sobbed the boy.

"Well, you can't, not now," said Bob, emphatically. "We hain't got no time for nonsense. You've either got to go along with me and Tom, and help us, or we will run you in. Now which will you do?"

The boy yielded to the eloquence of the chief detective, and accompanied him and Tom back to old Gunwagner's. The boldness of this move captured young Flannery's admiration.

"Now this is what I call bein' detectives, Bob," whispered he. "Gewhittaker, I didn't think, though, you could do it so grand. I don't believe nobody could beat you."

Bob nodded his approval of the compliment, and then addressed himself to the young lad.

"I want you," said he, "to take me in and say I'm a friend of yours who wants to sell somethin'. You needn't do nothin' more. Every detective puts up jobs like this, so 'tain't tellin' nothin' wrong."

Then, turning to his companion, he added:

"Now, Tom, if this boy ain't square, and he does anything so I get into Gunwagner's clutches, and can't get out, why I want you to go for an officer, and come and arrest this boy and the whole gang."

The lad trembled. "I won't do nothin'," he protested. "I'll do just what you want me to."

"All right; you do so, and you'll save yourself a visit to the Island. Now, when I am talking with old Gunwagner, if I tell you to come outside and get the package I left at the door, why, you come jest as if I did have it there, and you come right straight for Tom, and he will tell you what to do. And mind you be sure and don't close the outside door, for I want you to leave it so you and Tom can get in without ringing the bell, for that's the secret of the whole job."

The boy readily assented to Bob's conditions and commands, and then the chief gave his companion secret instructions, to be acted upon after he himself had gone into the very den of the old fence.

CHAPTER XIII.

A TERRIBLE FEAR.

IT was towards morning when Herbert Randolph fell asleep on the night of his imprisonment. He had fought manfully to keep awake, dreading the consequences of slumber, but tired nature gave way at last, and our young hero slept, unconscious now of danger.

The rats that he so much feared still frolicked, and prowled, and gnawed, as they had done for hours. They climbed upon boxes and barrels, and made their way into every corner and crevice. Everything was inspected by them.

More inquisitive rats than these never infested the metropolis. Now they went in droves, and scampered from place to place like a flock of frightened sheep. Then they strayed apart and prowled for a time alone. An occasional fight came off by way of variety, and in these battles the vanquished, and perhaps their supporters, often squealed like so many young pigs.

Thus the carousal continued hour after hour, and that old Gunwagner cellar was for the time a diminutive bedlam. Our young hero, nevertheless, slept on and on, unconscious of this racket.

After a while the rats grew bolder. Their curiosity became greater, and then they began to investigate more carefully the state of things within the prison cell, and at length their attention was turned to the quiet sleeper.

Well bred rats are always cautious, and therefore are somewhat respectful, but the drove at old Gunwagner's did not show this desirable trait. In fact they were not unlike the old fence himself—daring, avaricious and discourteous. No better proof of this could be instanced than their disreputable treatment of our young hero.

Rats, as a rule, show a special fondness for leather. Undoubtedly it is palatable to them. But this fact would not justify them in the attempt they made to appropriate to themselves Herbert's boots. The propriety of such an act was most questionable, and no well mannered rats would have allowed themselves to become a party to such a raid. But as a matter of fact, and as Herbert learned to his sorrow, there were no well mannered rats at old Gunwagner's—none but a thieving, quarrelsome lot.

After a council of war had been held, and a great amount of reconnoitering had been done, it was decided that these rural boots could not be removed from their rightful owner in their present shape; therefore they fell vigorously to work to reduce them to a more movable condition.

When Herbert fell asleep, he was sitting on a bench with his feet upon the floor. He was still in this position, with his head resting in his hand, and his elbow supported by the side of his prison cell, when the rats made war on his boots. They gnawed and chipped away at them at a lively rate, and in a little time the uppers were entirely destroyed. The cotton linings, to be sure, were still intact, as these they did not trouble. Evidently cotton cloth was not a tempting diet for them.

Up to this time Herbert had not moved a muscle since he

fell asleep, but now a troubled dream or something else, I know not what, disturbed him. Possibly it was the continued gnawing on his already shattered boots. It might, however, have been the fear of these dreadful rats, or the repulsive image of old Gunwagner, that haunted him and broke the soundness of his slumbers.

Presently he opened his eyes, drowsily, and his first half waking impression was the peculiar sensation at his feet. In another instant a full realization of the cause of this feeling darted into his mind, and with a pitiful cry of terror he bounded into the air like a frightened deer. And to add to the horror of his situation, in descending his right foot came down squarely upon one of the rats, which emitted a strange cry, a sort of squeal, that sent a thrill throughout every nerve of our hero's body.

A second leap brought him standing upon the bench upon which he had been sitting.

If ever a boy had good reason to be frightened, it was Herbert Randolph. His situation was one to drive men mad —in that dark, damp cellar, thus surrounded and beset by this countless horde of rats. The cold perspiration stood out upon him, and he trembled with an uncontrollable fear.

Something was wrong with his feet. He knew that, for his shoes now barely hung upon them. To what extent the rats had gone he dreaded to know. Already he could feel his feet smart and burn in a peculiar manner. Had they received poisonous bites, he asked himself? The mere suggestion of such a condition to one in his frightened state of mind was quite as bad, for the time, as actual wounds would have been.

A rat isn't very good company at any time. Under the most favorable conditions his presence has a tendency to send

SUDDENLY REALIZING HIS HORRIBLE SITUATION, HERBERT SPRANG UPON THE BENCH WITH A PITIFUL CRY OF TERROR.

people upon chairs or the nearest table, and not infrequently they do this little act with a whoop that would do credit to a genuine frontier Indian. When, therefore, we consider this fact, it is not difficult to realize the alarming situation in which our young hero was, and but for the timely sound of footsteps overhead it is impossible to predict what might have been the result of this terrible mental strain on him.

The night had worn away, the old fence was again on the move, and Herbert's piercing cry brought him to the room over the cell. No sooner had our young friend heard this sound above his head than he appealed for help. So alarming were his cries that even old Gunwagner was at length moved to go to his assistance. He retraced his steps to the front of the house, and, taking a lighted lamp with him, passed down through the trap door, and then made his way into the rear cellar to Herbert's cell.

Never before in his life had the presence of a human being been so welcome as was that of Gunwagner to our frightened hero. What a relief to this oppressive darkness was that small lamp light, and how quickly it drove all the rats into their hiding places.

"What's all this row about?" growled the old fence.

"These rats," gasped Herbert, with a strange, wild look; "see, they have bitten me," pointing to his boots, or what remained of them.

Gunwagner's heart softened a trifle as he beheld the boy's sufferings, and saw how he had been assailed.

"Are you sure they have bit you?" said he, uneasily.

"Look! see!" replied Herbert, holding out the worst mutilated boot. He fully believed he had been bitten, though, as a matter of fact, he had not.

The old fence became alarmed, fearing the annoyance and possible danger that might follow; but when he had satisfied himself by a careful examination that young Randolph had sustained no injuries, he speedily changed back to his old hard manner again—a cold, cruel manner that showed no mercy.

Herbert begged to be released from his prison pen, but his pleadings were of no avail.

"Why are you treating me in this inhuman way?" asked he. "What have I done that I should be shut up here by you?"

Old Gunwagner looked hard at him, but made no reply.

"I know why it is," continued our hero, growing bold and defiant when he saw it was useless to plead for kindness; "I can see through the whole scheme now; but you mark my words, old man, you will suffer for this cruelty, and so will your friend Felix Mortimer."

These words came from the lips of the young prisoner with such terrible emphasis that old Gunwagner, hardened as he was in sin, grew pale, and trembled visibly for his own safety.

CHAPTER XIV.

BOB OUTWITS THE OLD FENCE.

BOB easily gained admittance to the den by the aid of his confederate. He found there old Gunwagner, Felix Mortimer, and another boy, who passed out just after the young detective entered. The old fence eyed Bob sharply, and perhaps somewhat suspiciously. The manner of the small boy was excited. He did not appear natural, and this alone was sufficient to attract the old man's attention.

It was a critical moment for Bob. He did not know that the boy would not turn against him. In fact, he half suspected he would, but nevertheless he was willing to take the chance in the interest of Herbert, and that he might do a skillful piece of detective work. Moreover, there was the danger of being recognized by Felix Mortimer, who had seen him twice that very day; once at the bank in the morning, and again in the afternoon when Bob played the role of bootblack.

Old Gunwagner questioned him sharply. The small boy, however, told the story precisely in accordance with Bob's instructions. The young detective meanwhile hastily surveyed the room and its furnishings, and when he had discovered what he thought would serve his purpose, he turned to his confederate, and said :

"Well, I believe I'll let this man have the things I brought with me. You may go out and get them, and bring them in here."

"Why didn't you bring them in with you?" asked the fence, suavely.

"I didn't know as we could trade, so I thought I'd better leave 'em outside," answered Bob, carelessly.

When Tom saw the boy come out alone, he knew the part he was to act, and following out the directions of his chief, he and the confederate rushed into the dark passageway leading to the fence, and yelled "Fire" with all the power they could command. Before giving the alarm, however, they lighted a newspaper, and placed it near the outer door.

Bob had purposely made his way to a far corner of the room, so that, as a matter of fact, he was farther from the place of exit than either Mortimer or Gunwagner. This was part of his scheme.

When the cry of fire reached the old fence, he bounded to the door like a frightened deer. Throwing it open, his eyes instantly fell upon the great flames that shot up from the burning paper. The sight struck terror to him, and, with an agonized cry, he rushed down the hallway to the immediate scene of the conflagration, with Felix Mortimer not far behind him.

A gust of wind now blew in through the partially open door, and scattered the charred remains of the newspaper all about the feet of the fence. In a few seconds all traces of the fire were lost, and then the trick dawned upon the old man. He was furious with rage, and ran out into the street, to try and discover the perpetrators of the deed.

Tom and the confederate remained on the opposite side of the street till Gunwagner and Mortimer appeared at the door. Bob had instructed Tom to do this.

Both Gunwagner and Felix tumbled into this trap, which, by the way, was a skillful one for our detective to set. As soon as they caught sight of the two boys, they started after them in hot pursuit, but Tom and the young lad were excellent runners, and, having a good start of their pursuers, they kept well ahead of them.

Seeing, therefore, that the chase was a hopeless one, the old fence and Mortimer returned to the den. The former was almost desperately ugly. He growled and raved in a frightful manner, that quite alarmed our young detective.

"What has become of that new boy?" asked Felix, who was the first to think about him.

Gunwagner was so thoroughly agitated that up to this time he had not thought about Bob. At young Mortimer's reminder, however, he stopped suddenly in his ravings, and the color as quickly left his face. Then he hurried to where a box containing silver and other valuables were kept.

"It's here," he gasped, almost paralyzed with the fear that it had been stolen by the strange boy.

"Is anything else missing?" asked Felix.

Our young detective was at this minute doubled up in a large box that was stowed away under a sort of makeshift counter. He had hurriedly concealed himself in this manner during the absence of the fence and Felix.

"I'll look things over and see," said old Gunwagner, replying to Mortimer's question.

Bob thought the game was all up with him now. He felt much as Tom Flannery did. He, too, "didn't want to be a detective, no how."

"There's no show for me if this old tyrant gets his hands on to me," said Bob to himself, as he lay cramped up in that dirty box, hardly daring to breathe. "I didn't think about it comin' out this way; if I had, I would a' fixed things with Tom different. Now I suppose he's gone home, as I told him to, and I can't look for no help from him or nobody else."

The situation was a depressing one, and it grew more so as the mousing old fence came nearer and nearer to where our young detective lay. He searched high and low for traces of theft, and examined everything with careful scrutiny.

He was now close to Bob's hiding place.

"He must be hid away here somewhere," said Felix, with a very anxious look upon his face.

"What makes you think so?" asked the old man, as he noticed young Mortimer's anxiety.

No boy ever tried harder to suppress his breath than Bob Hunter did at this instant. "It's

GUNWAGNER PURSUING THE BOYS.

all up with me now," said he to himself. "They'll get me sure; but I'll die game."

"It looks suspicious to me, and that's why I think so," replied Felix, showing no little alarm.

"I don't see nothing suspicious about it, as long as nothing is missing."

"To be sure, but I believe he is the same boy that was in the bank today looking for this Randolph."

"And he is the boy that the old banker told you about?"

"Yes; the newsboy who said some foul play had overtaken Randolph."

The old fence looked exceedingly troubled.

"We must capture this young Arab," said he, emphatically, after a few moments' careful thought.

Bob's ears missed nothing. This conversation interested him through and through.

"Arab!" said he to himself. "If I don't get caught I'll show you whether I'm an Arab or not."

"Perhaps he is already in there," suggested Mortimer again.

"We will go down cellar and see," said the old man. "He might have gone down through that trap door while we was out."

"That's what I thought; and he and Randolph may already be hatching up some plan for escaping," said Felix.

Why old Gunwagner neglected to search the big box under the counter is inexplicable. Possibly the hand of destiny shielded the young detective, for he was on an errand of mercy.

The old man and Felix now descended the stairs into the cellar, and commenced their search for the strange boy who had so thoroughly alarmed them.

CHAPTER XV.

BOB AND HERBERT MEET.

"WELL, I can't understand it," said Felix, as he and the old fence came up from the cellar. "He certainly isn't down there."

"No, he ain't here, that's sure," replied Gunwagner; "but if it was the newsboy, you can be sure he will show up again in a way not very good for us."

"So I think," assented Mortimer.

"Then we must capture him, that's all."

"I wish we could. You see he might go to old Goldwin again, and tell him he saw me here."

"Yes, or go to the police headquarters and raise a row," suggested Gunwagner, gloomily.

"I didn't think of that. Well, as you say, the only thing for us to do is to capture him and get him where he won't make trouble for us."

"The whole game will be lost, and we will be pulled by the police unless we do so."

"You might's well count your game lost, then," said Bob to himself, for he had now renewed hope of carrying through his scheme. But he was nearly paralyzed with pain, from the cramped and uncomfortable position in which he had remained so long. He felt, however, that he was doing a great detective act, so he bore up under his sufferings with heroic fortitude.

"Suppose the police should drop on us, and find Randolph in the cellar?" suggested young Mortimer.

The thought evidently alarmed old Gunwagner. His face and whole manner showed that it did.

"If they should do that, we would go to Sing Sing," returned he, grimly.

Felix Mortimer possessed an extremely cool nerve, but the words "Sing Sing" did not fall upon his ears like sweet music.

"I wish we could get him out of the way," said he, with manifest anxiety. "It must be done tomorrow."

"There's no time to lose, I feel sure. But what shall be done with him?"

"He must be put where he will never blow on us."

"Of course he must."

"It's a bad job—a dirty, bad job—that's what I call it. I only wish you'd kept away from me with your devilish scheme," said the old villain, petulantly.

"It's no time to talk about that now," returned Mortimer, coolly. "You are in for it as well as I, so we must work together."

"We must, must we?" hissed the old man, wickedly.

"Yes," said Mortimer, with a determined manner, that made the old outlaw cower and cringe. Felix Mortimer possessed the stronger character of the two, and, now he was aroused, Gunwagner was subservient to his will.

"Unless you show yourself a man now, I will leave you to fight it out alone," continued Felix. "I can take care of myself. Randolph is on your hands, and here the police will find him."

Low, profane mutterings from the old culprit's mouth now filled the air. He was cornered, and Mortimer had him at his mercy. Gunwagner saw this now, and commenced planning to get our young hero out of the way.

An exceedingly interesting conversation this proved to the young detective, who carefully gathered in every word.

"Something is liable to drop with you fellers before long," said he to himself. "This detective business is mighty excitin', if it's all like this is. I wonder what Tom Flannery would say now, if he could take this all in the same way I'm doin' it!"

"I s'pose we can run him off to sea," said Gunwagner, at length. "That's the only way I know of to get him out of the way."

"Then why not do that?" replied Mortimer.

"It will cost a lot of money."

"Better pay out the money than go to Sing Sing."

The old fence looked daggers at the author of this remark, but evidently thought it best to make no direct reply.

"I wish we could get him away tonight," continued young Mortimer, in a way that exasperated Gunwagner.

"Well, you're mighty liable to be accommodated," thought Bob, as a broad grin played over his face, despite the suffering he was enduring. "I'm goin' to take a hand in this business myself, and I'll try my best to help you fellers through with this job."

"No, it can't be done tonight," said the old fence, gruffly; "but I'll see what can be done tomorrow."

"Fix it so he will never get back here to New York again," said Mortimer, heartlessly.

"Of course; that's the only thing to do."

"Remember, there is no time to lose, for if we get tripped

up here, the whole game will be up at the bank, and all our trouble will come to nothing."

"I understand that; but you have said nothing about the outlook at the bank."

"I have had no chance. Some one has been here all the evening."

"You have the chance now."

"So I have; but there is nothing to say yet. You don't expect me to rob a bank in one day, do you?"

"No, of course not; but what are the chances for carrying out the scheme?"

"Ah, ha!" said the young detective to himself; "bank robbing, is it? That's the scheme. Well, this detective business beats me. I guess nobody don't often get a more excitin' case than this one is—that's what I think."

After a little further discussion between the two crooks, Mortimer left the den and started for home. Bob suspected that he felt very happy to get away from there; and Bob was quite right, for, as a matter of fact, the young scoundrel had become so alarmed over the prospect, that he felt very uneasy about remaining a minute longer than was absolutely necessary. When he had gone, the old fence closed and bolted the doors, and then passed into a rear room, where he retired to his bed.

When all had been quiet for perhaps the space of fifteen or twenty minutes, the young detective crawled out of his box and straightened himself out. He had, however, been cramped up so long that this was not so easily done. But matters of so great moment were before him now, that he could not think of aches and pains. He learned about the location of the trap door, when the old fence and young Mortimer went into the cellar to look for him.

On his hands and knees Bob cautiously proceeded, searching on either side of him for the door. It was so dark that he could see nothing, and as the room was filled with chairs, old boxes, and so on, he found it no easy matter to navigate under such circumstances, especially as he knew that the slightest noise would prove fatal to his scheme.

At length his hand rested upon the fastening of the trap door, and to his horror he found it locked. If the room had seemed dark before to the young detective, it was now most oppressively black. What to do, which way to turn, he did not know. The doors leading to the street were locked, he had no keys about him, and no means of producing a light.

"This is the worst go I've struck yet," said Bob to himself, as he meditated over his situation. "Jest as I thought everything was all fixed, this blamed old lock knocks me out. Well, I've pulled through pretty good so far, and I won't give it up yet. I may strike an idea," he continued, undismayed, and then commenced prowling stealthily about the room, in search of something—anything that would serve his purpose.

He thought if he could find the key to the hall door he would try to make his escape from the building; and, once out, he could get matches, and whatever else he needed to aid him in carrying out his scheme to a grand success. But he was no more fortunate in this effort than he had been in hunting for the key to the trap door.

He searched, too, every nook and corner for a match, but failed utterly to find one, or anything to keep his courage good. The situation began to look alarming to him. He was now as much a prisoner as Herbert Randolph.

"I wonder what Tom Flannery would do if he was in my place?" mused the young detective, as he sat upon the floor, somewhat depressed in spirits. "I think he'd just lay down and bawl and throw up the whole game, that's what Tom Flannery would do. But I ain't goin' to throw up no game till it's lost, not ef Bob Hunter knows himself. There ain't but one thing to do now, and that's to go into old Gunwagner's bedroom, and take them keys outer his pocket, that's what I think. Ef he was to wake up, tho', and catch me at it—well, I guess I wouldn't be in the detective business no more. But — what's that noise?" said he to himself, suddenly becoming aware of a strange sound.

Our young detective felt a cold chill creep over him. His first thought was that the old fence was coming into his presence, and would of course capture him and punish him most inhumanly. But as the slight noise continued, and Gunwagner did not appear, Bob took courage, and listened keenly for developments. Presently the sound came nearer, and now a gleam of light shone up through a crack in the floor.

"Can it be Vermont?" said Bob to himself, hardly believing his own eyes.

Still nearer came the light.

"He is climbing the stairs, as sure's I'm alive," said Bob, almost overcome with joy.

In the trap door was a small knot hole, about an inch and a half in diameter. Through this opening the light now shone distinctly, and it was most welcome to the eyes of our young detective. A pressure was now brought to bear upon the door from the under side, but it only yielded so far as the fastening would allow.

"Is that you, Vermont?" whispered Bob through the knot hole.

No answer was given.

Herbert Randolph had never considered himself in any degree superstitious. But what could this be but Bob Hunter's spirit?

"Don't be afraid," said the young detective, who imagined Herbert would find it difficult to realize that he was there. "It's Bob Hunter. I ain't got no card with me, or I'd send it down to you."

This remark sounded so much like Bob that young Randolph no longer doubted his own senses.

"Bob Hunter!" exclaimed he. "How in the world came you here, and what are you doing?"

"Yes, it's me, Vermont. But don't stop to ask no questions now. I'm here to help you get out, but this blamed old door is locked, and I hain't got no key, nor no light, nor nothin'."

After exchanging a few words, Herbert took from his pocket a piece of paper. This he made into a taper, which he lighted and passed up through the knot hole to Bob. With this the latter lighted the gas; and now he felt that he was in a position to be of some service to his friend.

A careful search failed to reveal any keys. Then the two boys discussed the situation, and presently Herbert passed a bent nail to the young detective, and instructed him how to operate on the lock, which speedily yielded to the boy's efforts. In another instant the trap door was thrown up, and, by a most unfortunate blunder, it fell back with a tremendous crash.

Herbert, however, emerged quickly from his cold, damp prison, with a look of consternation pictured upon his face. Both he and Bob knew that old Gunwagner would be upon them in less than a minute, and they hastily prepared to defend themselves.

CHAPTER XVI.

THE OLD FENCE IN A TRAP.

"WHAT shall we do?" said Bob, with no little alarm, as Herbert Randolph climbed up through the old trap door.

"We must defend ourselves," replied the young Vermonter, with characteristic firmness.

"There ain't no way to escape, is there?"

"No, I suppose not, if the hall door is locked."

"It is, and I can't find no key."

"Have you looked since the gas was lighted?"

"Yes, and 'tain't there nowhere."

"Where do you imagine it is?"

"I guess the old duffer has it in his pocket, the same as he has the key to the trap door."

"Well, there is no time to lose. Old Gunwagner will be down upon us in an instant."

"Do you think he will bring a revolver with him?" asked Bob, somewhat nervously.

"Very likely he will."

"I guess we'd better climb down cellar, then, and pretty lively, too."

"No, we won't," replied Herbert, decidedly. "I have had all of that prison I want. We will fight it out here."

" All right, then, I'll shut this door down, or we might get thrown down cellar in the fight."

" So we might, and—— Ah, here he comes ! " said young Randolph, detecting the sound of footsteps, as old Gunwagner approached.

GUNWAGNER BURSTS INTO THE ROOM IN A FURIOUS MOOD.

" Stand in front of the counter, so that he will see you when he opens the door, and——"

" But the revolver ! " interrupted Bob.

He had now entirely relinquished the leadership, for in Herbert Randolph he recognized his superior.

" I was going to tell you about that," replied our hero.

"If you see a revolver in his hand, you must drop behind the counter as quickly as possible."

"Yes, and I won't waste no time about it, either."

"No, you'd better not," said the young Vermonter; and he had barely time to dart behind the door, when old Gunwagner placed his hand upon the latch, and burst into the room. His eye fell upon Bob Hunter, who stood directly in front of him, but about two thirds of the way across the room.

The old fence recognized him instantly, and with a fiendish shout made for the lad, as if he meant annihilation. He had not proceeded far, however, when young Randolph bounded from behind the door, and fell upon his shoulders, bearing him to the floor.

A yell of terror escaped from the old villain, that told clearly of his alarm. He had not thought of Herbert until now. He was at a loss to know what caused the noise, when the trap door slipped back with such a resounding crash.

But when his eyes fell upon Bob Hunter, he readily jumped at the conclusion that he alone had caused the rumpus. Now, however, he was stunned at this unexpected assault from the rear. When Herbert and the old man fell to the floor, Bob Hunter was quickly at his friend's side, ready to take a hand in the struggle, if needed.

While old Gunwagner was a cruel, heartless man, he nevertheless lacked genuine courage. Like the majority of men of his class, he was a coward at heart. He therefore readily gave up the struggle, when surprised by Herbert Randolph.

"It's your turn now, old man," said our young hero, triumphantly. "Last night you pounced upon me, and seemed to like it. Now perhaps you will enjoy this!"

A coarse oath, characteristic of the old villain, was the reply.

"You may as well submit decently. You are in our power now, and if you behave yourself, you will save us the necessity of compelling you to obey."

The old fence grated his teeth, and looked the very incarnation of all that was evil. The wicked spirit that shone in his face would have afforded a rare study for a painter. He made a movement of his right hand, as if to reach back to his hip pocket. A movement of this sort, under such circumstances, is considered suggestive of firearms.

Bob did not wait to see whether he was reaching for a revolver or some other ugly weapon, but instantly fell upon this hand, and secured it. The other hand was in Herbert's firm grasp, so it was useless for the old fence to struggle further.

"My turn has come now to get square with you, you cruel old sinner," said Herbert. "I begged of you to take me out of that foul cellar and away from those dreadful rats, but you showed no mercy."

Gunwagner made no reply.

"Yes, and he was goin' to send you off on some kind of a ship tomorrow, so you would never get back to New York no more," said Bob.

"Send me off on a ship!" exclaimed our hero, with a shudder. He had not until now even imagined the full purpose of his enemies.

"Yes, that's what they said tonight, him and that Mortimer feller."

"And you heard this?"

"Yes, when I was in that box under the counter there," replied Bob, with enthusiasm; "and they talked about bank robbin', too."

At this revelation old Gunwagner seemed to give up all

hope. The hardness of his face melted into an expression of pain, and he trembled with fear, like the frightened thing that he was. He had been outwitted by the young detective.

"Richard Goldwin's bank, I suppose," replied young Randolph, almost dazed at the audacity of the villains.

"Yes, that was their game in getting you out of the way."

"I didn't think of that before."

"Well, you hain't been in New York very long, and so you don't know the way they do things here—them that is bad, like this gang."

"How did you find out where I was, and how in the world did you manage to get in here without being seen?"

"Well, you see, I was a detective," said Bob, with a show of pride.

"A detective!" exclaimed the young Vermonter, looking at his friend with the innocent wonder of a country boy.

"Yes, but I hain't got no time to tell you about it now. We must be movin', you see."

"So we must," replied Herbert.

Doubtless old Gunwagner, too, would have liked much to hear Bob relate how he discovered his friend's prison. But even this small satisfaction was denied him.

"What's the first move?" said Bob.

"I have been thinking about that," replied our hero.

"Of course, we must have him arrested."

"Certainly we must."

"Oh, no, don't, don't!" pleaded the old man, speaking for the first time.

"It is too late to plead now," said young Randolph. "You should have thought of this before committing the evil that you have done."

"But I am an old man, and he led me into it."

"Who?"

"Mortimer, Felix Mortimer. If it hadn't been for him, I wouldn't er done it."

"Oh, that don't go with us," said Bob. "I heard the whole story tonight. You was into the game with him, and now you're trapped you wanter squeal, that's what you do. But it won't do you no good. You are a bad lot from way back—gettin' boys to steal things for you!"

This was a revelation to young Randolph, as he did not know until now that old Gunwagner kept a fence.

"Don't have me arrested, boys," whined the old villain, now trying to work on their sympathy. "It would kill me. I am so old."

"Do you expect sympathy from me, after your heartless treatment?" said Herbert.

"He made me do it," was the reply, referring to Mortimer.

"Nonsense, you could have taken me out of that old cellar if you had wanted to do so."

"Yes, and do you think you would er showed me any sympathy, if you'd got me into your clutches alone?" put in Bob.

"I wouldn't have been hard on you."

"No, you wouldn't," said the young detective, sarcastically. "Your talk tonight, when I was hid away, sounded as if you wouldn't er been hard on me—oh, no, you wouldn't. I could tell that from the way you plunged at me just now, when you came through that door with your war paint on."

CHAPTER XVII.

BOB GOES FOR AN OFFICER.

OLD Gunwagner saw quite clearly that any further effort to play upon the boys' sympathy was useless.

The first shock of his surprise was over, and now the subtle cunning of his nature began to reassert itself.

"Boys, you have the advantage of me at present," said he, softly. "But I can't see how it will pay you to act foolish."

"What do you mean?" asked Herbert.

"I mean that it will pay you a good deal better to make terms with me."

"How so?"

"Would you like to be rich?" was the reply.

"I suppose every American wants to be rich, and I guess we are no exception, are we, Bob?"

"I should think we ain't," replied the latter.

"So I thought," said the old fence, "and it's in my power to make you rich."

The boys were listening to subtle, dangerous words.

"How can you do that?" said Bob, growing interested.

"There are a number of ways that I might do it. In the first place, I could give both of you all the money you will ever need, and still be rich myself."

"But a man isn't likely to give away so much," said Herbert.

"You must have a payin' business," observed the young detective.

"Of course I must, and that is the point I am coming at. You boys have shown yourselves keen lads, and I always like to help such boys along, for I was poor once myself. Now my proposition is this: I'll give you both a show in the business here with me."

"No, sir, thank you, we do not care to go into a dishonest business like this," said Herbert, emphatically, speaking for both Bob and himself.

"Not if you could each make ten thousand a year, clean money?"

"No; not if we could make ten times that," replied our hero.

"You could have a good time on ten thousand a year—boys of your age."

"Not on stolen money."

"It wouldn't be on stolen money."

"It looks very much like it, when you buy stolen goods."

"Yes, and fix up a job for bank robbin'," added Bob.

"Well, suppose it does look so, why couldn't you enjoy the money just as much?"

"Because it wouldn't be right for us to have it," returned our hero.

"Boys, you are not so old as I am. I've seen a good deal of life. Money is money, and it don't matter where it comes from, it will buy just as much."

"It will not always buy one his liberty," replied young Randolph, coolly.

This remark came close home to the old fence, and disconcerted him for a minute. Presently, however, he rallied, and said:

"Do you think one has his liberty, as you call it, when he is poor—so poor that he can have no luxuries?"

"To be sure he does. Why not?"

"You will change your mind some day, and perhaps it will be too late."

"I hope I shall never change my mind in favor of dishonesty and crime."

"Do you know that a boy's chance to get rich hardly ever comes to him but once in his life?" continued old Gunwagner, undaunted.

"No, and I don't believe it is so, either."

"Another evidence of your inexperience. When you get older, you will look back and see what I tell you is true; and if you miss this chance you will never get another one like it."

"We don't want another one like it, so it's no use to talk about it any more."

"That's so," said Bob; "he hain't got no interest in us; I can see through his trick."

"You are mistaken, young man. If you don't want to go into the business here yourselves, I'll give you an interest in it, if you will do nothing to injure it. You see, you know about the business here now, and if you should give it away to the police, why it would hurt it, don't you understand?"

"Yes, we understand it too well, but do not want an interest in it," said Herbert.

"It would pay you well," persisted the old fence; "say about seven to ten thousand dollars each every year, and you needn't come anear it—just take your dividends every week, and that's all."

"Well, we don't want no such dividends," said Bob; "nor we couldn't get 'em if we did want 'em, that's all."

"You are mistaken again, for if you think the business don't pay as well as I say, why I can show you the money."

"Got it with you?" said Bob.

This question pleased the old fence, and gave him renewed courage. He thought now that perhaps there was yet hope for him.

"I have it in the house," said he.

"In cash?"

"Yes, and I can get it if you want to see it."

"Don't see how you're goin' to get it, the way you are fixed now," continued Bob.

"Well, if you will not let me go for it, I can tell you where to find it."

"Can you? Well, where is it?"

"It is in my bedroom, in the further end of the house. You will find it in the thick wallet, under my pillow."

"Well, we will take your word for it, seein' we don't need the money for anything, and wouldn't take it nohow," said the young detective, who divined the purpose of the old fence.

"But if you don't get it, how can I make you boys a present? You will not allow me to go for it," said the fence, fearing his scheme had failed him.

"We don't want no present, so don't worry yourself about that."

"We prefer taking you with us, rather than the present," said Herbert.

"Old man," continued Bob, "your game didn't work. All you wanted was to get me out of the way so you could er layed Vermont out. But it warn't no go. You was too anxious to give away money. I could see all the time what you was aimin' at."

The old fence protested against this interpretation of his motives, but the boys were too keen for him. Young Bob Hunter had been knocking about the streets of New York too long to be very easily taken in by this old Gunwagner. His wits had been sharpened to a high degree in his long struggle for bread, and his knowledge of human nature was as superior to that of Herbert Randolph as the latter's general education was superior to Bob's.

GUNWAGNER IN THE HANDS OF THE POLICE.

Finding it impossible to work upon the sympathy of the boys, that buying them off was out of the question, and that the scheme to outwit them had proved a flat failure, Gunwagner now turned to the last weapon which he could hope to use with any possible effect.

"So you have made up your mind to take me with you?" said he, looking hard at Herbert.

"Yes," replied the latter, firmly.

"You will make the biggest mistake of your life, if you attempt such an outrage."

"An outrage! Is that what you call it, when a detective takes a bird like you in?" said Bob Hunter, in his characteristic manner.

The old fence looked fiercely at him.

"My friends are all around here, and I can raise a dozen of them before you could get me half a block away."

"We do not feel uneasy about your so called friends," said young Randolph. "But if you prefer it, we will send for an officer, and let him take you."

"If your friends go back on you the way Mortimer done tonight, when he told you he would look out for himself, and let you fight it out alone, why, then I guess me and Vermont needn't bother much about your gang."

Further intimidation was tried by Gunwagner, but all to no purpose, for now the boys were in the act of fastening together the wrists of the old fence, and binding them securely to a chair. When this had been done, so that they no longer felt any insecurity, they took from his pocket the keys to both doors leading to the street, and Bob Hunter started for an officer. Young Randolph remained with the prisoner, because he was stronger than Bob, and therefore would be the better able to handle him, should he by any means get his hands loose.

Now every hope had failed the old man. He saw nothing

but Sing Sing before him. His evil purpose had at last recoiled upon him, and he was a prisoner in the hands of one who but a few hours before had begged of him for mercy.

While waiting for the return of Bob with the officer, Herbert asked Gunwagner if the money he had made in crooked and unlawful ways had brought him happiness. He made no audible reply, but sat with his head bent low. An answer, however, was conveyed to our young hero by a silent tear that made its way slowly down the wrinkled and aged face of the old man, whose life had been worse than wasted, for it had been an evil one.

CHAPTER XVIII.

TOM FLANNERY IS HUNGRY.

IT was past midnight when Herbert Randolph and Bob Hunter reached their room. The old fence had meanwhile been taken to the station house by an officer. Both boys were sleepy and well nigh exhausted, so they immediately sought rest.

Bob, however, was up at his usual hour in the morning, and off to look after his paper trade. Business proved good with him on this occasion—unusually good—so that his profits amounted to quite a nice little sum. He therefore planned to give Herbert a good warm breakfast, something better than it had been their custom to eat.

Presently Tom Flannery appeared.

"You here, Bob?" said the latter, with surprise. "I thought you was done for, sure."

"What made you think that, Tom?"

"Why, because you didn't show up."

"You didn't wait for me, did you?"

"Didn't I? Well, I should think I did, till near twelve o'clock, too, when I was so near froze I couldn't stay no longer; and Bob, I thought it was all up with you."

"Why, Tom, you hadn't oughter staid. I told you to go home after you lit the fire."

"I know you did, Bob, but I didn't feel like goin' home and leavin' you alone in that den. You see I thought you might need me."

"Tom, you've got more sand than I thought you had. I wish I coulder fixed it so you coulder been on the inside too."

"I wish you could, Bob. Was it excitin'?"

"Excitin'! Well, wasn't it, though! I never saw anything like it. But I say, Tom, that was a great go. You done it splendid."

"What's that, Bob?"

"Why, the fire act. I don't believe nobody could beat that."

Tom enjoyed this praise hugely.

"I wouldn't like to a' been in your place, Bob," said he, "when you was in that dark room, nor when old Gunwagner and that other feller was huntin' for you."

"No, I thought you wouldn't, Tom, and I didn't want to be there neither."

"'Twas a big detective job, wasn't it, Bob?"

"Well, 'twas a pretty fair one, I guess."

"And you got it all up yourself," continued Tom, admiringly. "I wish I could do things the way you do, Bob."

"Well, you see, Tom, you hain't had so much experience as what I have, but you'll come out all right, and make a big detective, I know you will."

Bob stopped talking to sell a paper, and after making change and pocketing his profit, he continued:

"Now, Tom, I tell you what 'tis: you and me and Herbert will eat breakfast together, when he comes down."

"When will he be down?" asked Tom, his hand dropping instinctively upon his empty stomach.

Tom Flannery was known among his crowd of street lads as the hungry boy. He was always ready to eat, and never seemed to get enough food to satisfy the cravings of his appetite. This invitation, therefore, was very welcome to him.

"It's 'bout time for him now," replied Bob, in answer to Tom's question.

"I wish he would come," said Tom, looking hungrier than usual.

"He is probably making up sleep," said the young detective.

"How much sleep has he got to make up, Bob?" asked Tom, seriously.

"I don't know exactly, but I guess pretty near a whole night."

"A whole night!" exclaimed Tom, dubiously. "He ain't goin' to make it all up this morning, is he, Bob?"

Tom's hand rested suggestively upon his stomach again.

"Shucks! Tom Flannery, if you ain't a idiot, I never saw one! To think Herbert Randolph would sleep all day! Didn't I tell you he would be right down?"

"So you did, Bob. I forgot that; but you see I wanted to be sure, cause I haven't had nothin' to eat yet today."

Bob looked at his companion with an air of disdain, and made no reply.

Tom, however, was not over sensitive, so he kept on talking about Bob's adventure at the fence. In the course of half an hour he got the whole story from the young detective. Bob not only told him his own adventures, but gave him all of Herbert's experience, which he had himself learned from our hero.

It was now about a quarter to nine. Tom looked suggestively at the big hands on the City Hall clock, but said nothing about young Randolph's non-appearance.

"I don't see what keeps him," said Bob, knowing full well what Tom was thinking about.

"Nor I don't either, Bob. I guess he won't be down very early."

"Well, there wasn't nothin' to bring him down early."

"But you expected him, didn't you, Bob?"

"Of course I did, Tom Flannery. Didn't I ask you to eat breakfast with me and him?"

"Yes, you did, Bob, and that was what I was thinking about."

"Well, what did you think about it?"

"I was wonderin' if you meant this mornin', or some other mornin'."

Tom had hardly finished this remark, when Herbert Randolph approached from the Broadway entrance and spoke to Bob.

"This is Tom Flannery, what helped me do the detective act," said the latter, by way of introduction. "You know I told you about him."

"Oh, yes, I remember, and I am glad to meet you, Tom Flannery," replied young Randolph, extending his hand to Tom.

"So am I glad to see you," said young Flannery; "me and Bob here have been waitin' for you more'n two hours."

"Oh, Tom Flannery!" exclaimed Bob. "What are you talkin' that way for? 'Tain't a quarter so much that we've been waitin', and you know it."

"Seems like 'twas a half a day to me, any way," protested Tom, with his hand again moving towards the seat of his digestion.

"The trouble is with Tom Flannery that he is always

starvin'. I never see such a hungry boy," explained the young detective.

"I can't help it," answered Tom; "I like to eat."

Bob explained to Herbert that they had been waiting for him to join them for breakfast.

"I am sorry," said young Randolph, "but I ate my breakfast on the way down."

Tom Flannery was disheartened.

"Never mind, Tom," said Bob; "we will have the breakfast some other mornin'—you and me and Vermont."

When it was time for Mr. Goldwin to get down to business, our hero and the young detective started for the banking house.

A surprise awaited Felix Mortimer.

CHAPTER XIX.

THE RIVALS AT THE BANK.

"DO you s'pose we will find that Mortimer feller at the bank?" asked Bob, as he and young Randolph passed down Broadway towards Wall Street.

"Very likely we shall," responded our hero, absent mindedly.

"If he has heard of old Gunwagner's arrest, you bet he won't be there."

"The papers contained nothing about the arrest, did they?"

"No, not as I seen."

"Then the chances are that he is there."

"So I think. But what will you do, Vermont, if he is?"

"I don't know yet."

"You won't lick him, will you?"

"Oh, no, that wouldn't be a wise policy to pursue."

"But he deserves it."

"So he does, but I can't afford to lower myself by fighting."

"That's so, Vermont; but, all the same, I'd like to see you lay him out once—the way you did at Gunwagner's—he deserves it."

"He deserves to be punished, but I think the law will do that."

"'Tain't quick enough," said Bob, petulantly. "A feller

gets all over his mad before he gets any satisfaction out of law."

"You are a comical chap, Bob," said Herbert; "but you have been one of the best friends I ever knew. If you had not come to my rescue, I should probably never have walked down this street again."

"Oh, that's all right," replied the young detective. "Don't say nothing about it."

The two boys had now reached the banking house of Richard Goldwin. Their conversation, therefore, terminated as they entered the bank.

Just as the door was opened to them, Mr. Goldwin came out of his private office, and his eyes fell upon Herbert and Bob.

"What do you mean, sir, by appearing in this bank again?" he asked, with a stern glance at young Randolph.

It must be remembered that he believed the story told to him by Felix Mortimer, and therefore looked upon Herbert with grave suspicions, or even contempt.

The banker's manner and implied insinuation wounded young Randolph's pride, and his cheeks became crimson.

"If you are not already prejudiced, I think, sir, I can explain to your entire satisfaction," said our young hero, with a native dignity well becoming his manliness.

"It's jest what I told you yesterday mornin'," put in Bob. "Foul play—that's what it was."

"I think I am not prejudiced to such an extent that I am incapable of dealing justly with you," replied Mr. Goldwin, giving no heed to Bob's remark.

"Thank you," said Herbert. "I am sure you are not, and if you will listen to me, I will explain everything."

"A mere explanation from you, however, will not convince me."

"It should do so," replied Herbert, still further wounded by this cold remark.

"Not at all, since you have deceived me once."

"I have never deceived you, sir," answered young Randolph, with spirit.

"Of course you would say so," returned the banker, coolly.

"Most certainly I would, sir, when I am telling you the truth."

"Have you any evidence to sustain your position?" asked Mr. Goldwin.

"Yes, sir," replied Herbert; "my friend here can testify that I have not deceived you. He knows the whole story—the plot from first to last."

Herbert Randolph's bold, straightforward manner impressed the banker favorably, and he now became less frigid towards him.

"There has evidently been deception somewhere," said Mr. Goldwin. "Why any one should plot against you, with a view to getting you out of this bank, I cannot understand."

"I think Bob Hunter here can make it plain to you. He knows the whole scheme."

"And it warn't no small scheme, neither," responded Bob. "It's lucky for you that we got on to it before it was too late."

"What do you mean by this insinuation, young man?"

"Well, if you want to know, I'll tell you. Perhaps you remember I was down here yesterday to see you, and I told you somethin' was wrong then—didn't I?"

"Yes."

"And you didn't believe it, but just talked against Herbert Randolph here."

"But I had good cause for doing so."

"Yes, if you think that stuff that Felix Mortimer give you was any cause, then you did have some; but he was jest lyin' to you, that's what he was doin', and I know it; and what's more, I can prove it," said Bob, boldly and bluntly.

"You are making a strong statement," replied the banker, somewhat bewildered.

"I know I am, but I couldn't say nothin' too strong about that Mortimer feller."

"Felix Mortimer is in my private office. Dare you come in and face him with these remarks?"

"You bet I dare—that's jest what I want to do."

"You shall do so, then," said the banker.

Herbert Randolph and Bob Hunter followed him, at his invitation, into his private room.

CHAPTER XX.

FELIX MORTIMER DISCOMFITED.

FELIX MORTIMER sat at a desk facing the door, and was writing when the banker and the two boys entered the room. He did not look up till Herbert and Bob had advanced several steps toward him, and stopped. But his eyes now met theirs, and he sprang to his feet like one suddenly surprised by a lurking enemy. Herbert and Bob stood there for a moment, boldly facing him. Not a word was spoken on either side.

The banker took a position where he could watch the effect of this strange meeting upon both parties. He saw the color fade from young Mortimer's face, and a look of unmistakable fear spread over it. In fact, his whole manner betrayed the alarm that now possessed him.

In strong contrast to the appearance of this young villain was Herbert Randolph's frank, truthful look. He had no cause for fear. The peculiar fire that shone in his eyes revealed a meaning that was at once impressive and determined. Before him stood one who had wronged him outrageously, stolen his position away from him, and blackened his character with ingenious falsehood.

Our hero thought of all this, and his blood boiled with manly indignation. Had he been alone with Mortimer, I fear the latter would have suffered then and there the penalty for his villainy. But discretion was now the sensible course for Herbert, and he wisely restrained himself from an unbecoming demonstration of hostility.

"Do you know these young men?" asked the banker, sharply, addressing young Mortimer.

"I know one of them, sir—that is, I saw him here the morning you advertised for a boy," replied Felix, commencing to rally.

"I recollect the fact. You refer to Herbert Randolph, I presume?"

"Yes, sir."

"I think you told me something about his getting another position, and this, you said, was probably the reason why he failed to continue working at this bank."

"Yes, sir," replied Mortimer, with bold effrontery.

"What have you to say to this young man's statement, Mr. Randolph?" said the banker.

Felix Mortimer's manner had already raised Mr. Goldwin's suspicions, but he wished to be doubly sure, and thus he proceeded carefully with the investigation.

"His statement is wholly false," was our hero's reply. "It was his miserable villainy that deprived me of my liberty, and kept me away from my work."

Mr. Goldwin looked puzzled.

"The plot thickens," said he. "Give me your story."

Herbert related how he had been victimized, telling the facts much as I have given them in the preceding chapters of this narrative.

"Tell him about the knock out," put in Bob, who evidently thought this one of the best parts of the story.

"What was that?" asked the banker.

Herbert explained.

"So that was what gave you the swollen jaw, was it?" said Mr. Goldwin, addressing Felix Mortimer in a severe tone.

"No, it was not," said he. "I told you what did it, and I don't propose to hear any more lies from street fellows like these," added Mortimer, contemptuously, and at the same time moving towards the door.

"Stop!" said the banker, firmly. "You will not leave this room till this matter is cleared up."

Young Mortimer winced, and Bob Hunter looked up at Herbert, and smiled suggestively.

"Mr. Randolph, this fellow stated to me yesterday that you were not from Vermont, that you are an impostor. What have you to say to this?"

"I can only say that I told you the truth."

"Have you any way of proving your statement?"

"Here is a letter that I received this morning from my mother," said Herbert, handing it to the banker. "This, I think, will sustain my word."

"The envelope is postmarked Fairbury, Vermont," replied Mr. Goldwin, scrutinizing it closely.

"You may read the letter," said our hero. "It will doubtless convince you of my truthfulness."

It ran as follows:

FAIRBURY, VT., Thursday, November 12th.

MY DEAR SON:

Your letter reached us this evening, and it lifted a great load of anxiety from our hearts, for we could not help fearing some ill luck might have overtaken you—a stranger and an inexperienced boy in so great a city as New York.

Your father and I rejoice at your good fortune, and feel proud that our boy should be chosen by the banker from among so large a number of applicants for the same position. Your excellent start gives us fresh courage to fight the battle of life over again, and to try and regain our property, or so much of it as will be necessary to support us comfortably in our old age.

Your father's eyes filled with tears of joy when I read your letter to him, and he said I might tell you that he feels rich in the possession of a son who has health, energy, and good principles, and who has shown himself able to make his way in the world unaided. He thinks you now have an excellent opportunity for commencing a prosperous career. From what you wrote of Mr. Goldwin, the banker, we think he must be a very nice man, and we are heartily glad that you can have his influence thrown about you to strengthen you against the evils you should shun.

We were greatly amused at the picture you gave of Bob Hunter the newsboy. You must find him very entertaining. Write us some more about him. His droll talk reads like a novel. Your father laughed heartily at it.

Be sure and write us two or three times a week, for you know we are entirely alone now you are away. With love from your father and myself, I will say good by for today.

YOUR MOTHER.

Mr. Goldwin commenced to read this letter aloud, but before he had finished it his voice choked, and he reached for his handkerchief with which to dry his moist eyes.

The picture it presented of the Vermont father and mother, so deeply interested in their only boy, brought fresh to the banker's mind his own parental home, and he saw himself once more bidding good by to his father and mother, as he left them and the old farm, a mere boy, to seek a livelihood in the great metropolis.

Presently he overcame this emotion, and turning to young Randolph, said, sternly:

"This letter, which I hold in my hand, not only proves Mr. Randolph's truthfulness, but it convicts you of a base falsehood. You deceived me by your artful lying, and now you have the effrontery to stand up before me and before this young man, whom you have so cruelly wronged, and boldly deny everything. You are the most polished young villain I ever knew.

"Young man," continued the banker, addressing Bob, and without waiting for Mortimer to reply, "what do you know about this matter?"

"I guess I know 'bout everything," said the young detective, glad of a chance to have his say.

"You remarked that it was lucky that you found out something before it was too late for us here at the bank, I believe?"

"Yes, sir, you are right."

"Will you please tell us the facts?"

Bob related the conversation he had heard between old Gunwagner and Felix Mortimer, relative to bank robbing.

"So that was your scheme in getting in here, was it? you young villain!" said Mr. Goldwin, angrily addressing Felix Mortimer.

"I refuse to answer the charges made by these confederates. They are telling what has no truth in it, and are deceiving you, as you will learn to your sorrow," replied Felix, still maintaining a good degree of boldness.

Richard Goldwin, however, was too good a judge of human nature to be further imposed upon by the tricks of young Mortimer.

"But you will be forced to answer to the charges sooner or later, sir," said the banker. "The court will compel you to do so."

The court!

These words made young Mortimer wince, and his nerve palpably weakened. He muttered some unintelligible reply—whether a threat or not none present knew.

"How came you to overhear this conversation between the old fence and this fellow?" asked Mr. Goldwin of Bob Hunter.

The young detective here related the whole story, telling why he suspected Mortimer, how he saw him at the bank in Herbert's place, how he shadowed him up Broadway—told of

YOUNG RANDOLPH AND BOB HUNTER CONFRONT FELIX MORTIMER AND CHARGE HIM WITH HIS VILLAINY.

the bootblacking scene, in which he got the essential facts from Peter Smartweed and Mortimer; related his manner of gaining admittance to the fence, and told of the trick he played upon the old man and Felix—the trick that enabled him to carry out to success his scheme for liberating Herbert Randolph.

"And you did all of this alone?" asked the banker, with genuine astonishment.

"Yes, sir," replied Bob, carelessly, as if it didn't amount to much.

"I cannot realize it," said Mr. Goldwin, admiringly. "A professional detective could not have done better, and probably would have fallen far short of doing as well."

"I didn't think nothin' of it," returned Bob. "'Twas easy enough, and 'twas kinder of excitin', too."

"And you liked the excitement?"

Bob admitted that he did, but was very modest about his triumph, and was not disposed to look upon it as any great feat now it was all over. But Mr. Goldwin assured him, in most complimentary terms, that great credit was due to him for the skill and bravery he had displayed.

Meanwhile Felix Mortimer had been slyly inching towards a door that was a little to his left; and now that Mr. Goldwin's attention was centered upon young Bob Hunter, he seized the opportunity, and made a mad plunge for liberty. His movements, however, had been detected by Herbert Randolph, and he no sooner reached the door than the young Vermonter grasped him firmly by the collar, and jerked him back.

Mortimer's effort to escape prompted Mr. Goldwin to sound the alarm for a policeman. An officer responded promptly, and immediately arrested the young criminal, and took him to the station house, where he was locked into a cell.

"I was never so deceived in a boy in my life," remarked the banker, with a troubled look, when the officer had gone with his prisoner. "He has a remarkably strong character, and had he taken the right course in life, would have made an able man. It always makes me sad to see a bright boy, just entering upon his career, start in a way that is sure to result in disgrace and ruin."

"His associates have doubtless had a bad influence over him," said Herbert, as if trying to soften the boy's offense.

"It is certainly praiseworthy in you, Mr. Randolph, to speak so kindly of one who caused you so much suffering as that boy did," returned Mr. Goldwin.

"Well, since his evil purpose has recoiled upon himself, he is now the chief sufferer; and besides, I do not think he wanted to injure me farther than to get me out of his way. And he knew no other plan, I suppose, than to keep me a prisoner."

"I am glad to see you view the matter so charitably," said the banker, warmly, for he appreciated highly this glimpse of Herbert's character.

"But what do you say to old Gunwagner?" put in Bob.

"I think he is a heartless old wretch," answered young Randolph, with fire in his eyes. "It is he who abused me so cruelly."

"You say he, too, is locked up now?" asked Mr. Goldwin.

"Yes."

"Do you think he has any property?"

"I should judge so. In fact, he tried to buy us off when he found we had him cornered."

"It is possible that you may be able to get damages for false imprisonment," said the banker, thoughtfully.

"I had not thought of that," returned Herbert.

"Mind you, I said it was possible only, so do not have too great hopes of such a result."

"No, I will not, and the damage was not much, unless I lost my situation with you," replied Herbert, somewhat anxiously.

"No, you have not lost that, for I shall reinstate you at once. You have proved yourself to be the sort of young man I desire in my business."

"Thank you, sir, for your compliment, and especially for reinstating me. I should be very sorry to lose this position, and I know my father and mother would feel badly, too."

"Do not worry about that, my boy. Employers are as anxious to get desirable clerks as clerks are eager to be employed. But to return to the matter of false imprisonment, I will state the case to my lawyer, and see what there is in it. Of course it would be no use to fight him if he is worth nothing."

"He said he had plenty of money—enough to make us all rich," put in Bob, with some enthusiasm. "It would be a great act to make him come down handsome. I'd like to see it done."

"Those fellows usually have a lot of money," said Mr. Goldwin, "and I agree with Bob—I will call you by that name hereafter—that it would be gratifying to recover damages."

"That's right, I like to be called Bob—everybody calls me that."

"Well, Bob, you are a character. I shall take a great interest in your development, for I think you have done the smartest thing, in getting your friend out of old Gunwagner's clutches, that I ever knew a boy of your age to do."

Bob's cheeks became highly colored. He had not been accustomed to praise, and such compliments as these from a rich banker were unwieldy for him.

"Tom Flannery helped me," said the young detective, generously trying to throw some of the glory upon Tom.

"Tom Flannery! Who is he?"

"He is a fellow what sells papers too. Me and him worked this case up together."

"What sort of a boy is he—sharp, like yourself, I suppose?"

"Well, he done some good work helpin' me," replied Bob, evading the question as to Tom's keenness.

The fact is that young Flannery was not wonderfully sharp; but Bob liked him for his honest, good natured self, and, therefore, would only speak in praise of him.

The banker drew Bob out, and learned of the fire act that Tom performed so satisfactorily. But his keen sense detected the truth of the matter, and he was satisfied as to where the real merit lay.

"Bob," said he, "your modesty and your efforts to throw much of the credit on Tom Flannery are certainly becoming to you. I like you for the spirit you show in the matter. But, nevertheless, I recognize in you the chief of the undertaking—the one who planned and carried out the entire scheme. Now, here is a little present for you; I want you to take it and buy you a good suit of clothes, so that you will be as well dressed as Herbert. I believe you room together?"

"Yes, we do," said Bob. "But I don't want no present. I can earn some money to buy clothes with."

"But I want you to take it," replied Mr. Goldwin. "You have done a great act of kindness to Herbert, and to me as well, for sooner or later we would doubtless have suffered a loss by Felix Mortimer."

Bob took the crisp new bills reluctantly—four of them, five dollars each—twenty dollars—he had never held so much money in his hands at any one time before, and this was all his own.

He felt bewildered. After a moment's pause, however, he said, "Mayn't I give some of this to Tom Flannery?"

"I expected you would say that," replied the banker, enjoying Bob's surprise, "so I retained a five dollar bill for Tom. Here it is; give it to him with my regards. He, too, did us a service in aiding you as he did."

Bob's joy was now beyond expression. He looked, however, the thankfulness that he could not find words to express.

"You may go now," said Mr. Goldwin, kindly. "I will keep you in mind, and see what I can do for you. Come and see me within a few days."

Bob thanked Mr. Goldwin heartily, and left the bank, overflowing with happiness. When the young detective had gone, Mr. Goldwin asked Herbert many questions about him.

"I think he is a promising lad," said the banker. "I have taken a great liking to him. He has a droll, comical way that is very pleasing."

CHAPTER XXI.

TWO YOUNG CAPITALISTS.

"IS that you, Bob Hunter?" said Tom Flannery, his eyes opened wide with surprise.

"I should think it is," laughed the young detective.

"Say, Bob, where did you get 'em?" continued Tom, somewhat in doubt of his own senses.

"Why, I bought 'em, of course. How does anybody get new clothes?"

"They are slick, though, ain't they, Bob?" said young Flannery, admiringly, "and they fit stunnin', too. You must er struck a snap somewhere, Bob."

"I should think I did," replied the latter; "the best snap any er the boys ever struck."

"Bob, you was always lucky. I wish I was as lucky as what you are. I never strike no snaps, Bob."

"Don't you?" said young Hunter, meditatively.

"No, they don't never come my way," responded Tom, dolefully.

Bob turned the lapels of his coat back and threw out his chest ponderously.

"Tom," said he, with the air of a Wall Street banker, "here's a five for you," taking a new, crisp bill from his vest pocket.

"For me, Bob!" exclaimed Tom, incredulously.

"Why, yes, of course it's for you. Why not?"

"I don't understand it, Bob," said young Flannery, completely upset.

"Why, it's one of them snaps. You said you never had any luck like me, so I thought I'd just give you some."

"Bob, you're a dandy. I never see any feller do things the way you do."

"Well, I do try to throw a little style into 'em, when it's handy to do it."

"I should think you do."

"You see, Tom, it don't cost no more to do things as they ought to be. I believe in doing 'em right, that's what I say."

"But, you see, Bob, believing in 'em and knowing how to do 'em is two dif-

"TOM," SAID BOB, "HERE'S A FIVE FOR YOU."

ferent things. Now I believe in 'em just the same as what you do, but I can't do 'em the same way."

"Well, you ain't so old, Tom."

"I know I ain't, but that don't make no difference, for when you was no older than what I am, why you done things in a awful grand way."

Bob here explained to Tom that the five dollar bill was a present to him from Richard Goldwin, the banker, and told him also about his own good luck.

"And he gave you all that money to buy these new clothes with! He is a bully old fellow, ain't he, Bob?" said Tom Flannery, greatly astonished.

"I should say so," responded Bob. "But I didn't spend it all, though."

"How much did you put up for 'em, Bob?"

"Fifteen dollars, that's all."

"They are swell, though, I tell you, Bob, and you look like kind of a masher," said Tom, criticising them carefully.

"Well, I ain't no masher, but I think myself they do look kinder slick."

"And you got five dollars left, too?"

"Yes, jest the same as what you have, Tom."

"What you goin' to do with it, Bob?"

"I hain't thought about that yet. What you goin' to do with yourn?"

"I guess I'll keep it, Bob, till next summer, and put it up on the races."

"What do you want to do that for, Tom Flannery?" returned Bob, with disgust.

"Why, to make some money, of course."

"Are you sure you will make it?"

"Of course I am, Bob. Nobody what knows anything at all can't lose when he has so much as five dollars to back him. It's them that don't have nothin' what gets broke on racin'."

"You know all about it, I suppose?"

"Why, of course I do, Bob; I've made a stake lots of times."

"And lost lots of times, too, I s'pose."

"Well, that's because I didn't have enough capital."

"But answer me this, Tom Flannery," said Bob, pointedly: "You admit you did get wiped out at bettin', do you?"

"Well, yes, I s'pose I did, Bob."

"And you'll get broke again, if you go at it. I tell you, Tom, they all get left, them that bets on horse racing."

"But don't some of them make slats of money? Answer me that."

"They don't make no money what sticks to 'em."

"What do you mean by that, Bob? I don't understand."

"I mean that they lose it the same way they make it, so it don't stick to 'em. Do you see?"

"Yes, I see. But how's a feller like me goin' to make any money, Bob, if he don't bet any?"

"Now, Tom, you're gettin' to somethin' I've been thinkin' about, and I'll let you into the secret. You see, Tom, I don't believe in horse bettin' the way you do, but I ain't afraid to take chances all the same."

"What is it, Bob?" interrupted Tom, eager to get into the secret.

"Wall Street," replied Bob, striking the attitude of a money king.

"Do you mean it, Bob?" asked young Flannery, incredulously.

"Of course I mean it, Tom. There's piles of money down there."

"I know there is, Bob, but how are fellers like you 'n' me going to get it?"

"Why, by speculatin', of course. How does any of 'em make it?"

"Them fellers are all rich, Bob. They didn't go down there the same as what we would go, with only five dollars," replied Tom.

"They didn't, did they? Well, tell me if Jay Gould, and the old man Sage, and half a dozen more of them big fellers, didn't go into Wall Street without a cent?"

"I can't tell you, Bob; I never heard anybody say," answered Tom, humbly.

"Well, Tom Flannery, I should think you would find out such things. Don't you never want to know anything?"

"I ain't been thinkin' about Wall Street, and them fellers you speak about, Bob," apologized Tom. "But I wish you'd tell me about 'em, for I'd like to know how they made their money."

"Well, I'll tell you some other time," said Bob, with assumed ease. As a matter of fact, however, he did not know himself, but was not willing to admit so much to Tom. He therefore decided to change the subject at once before getting cornered.

"Now, Tom," he continued, "I'll tell you what it is. I've jest thought what we'll do, you 'n' me and Herbert."

"What is it, Bob?"

"Well, you see we got knocked out of our breakfast this morning, Tom, so I think the best thing we can do is to have a big dinner tonight."

"I think so too, Bob," said Tom, eagerly.

"You see, 'twould be a celebration of the way we worked the detective business."

"So 'twould, Bob. That's a good idea, I think."

"I think so, too, Tom, and we'll have a regular first class lay out."

"It will be immense, Bob, I know 'twill," said Tom, with enthusiasm. "I never had a big dinner, Bob."

"No, I should think you never did, but you won't be hungry, Tom, when you get done with the one we will have to-night."

"I hope I won't, Bob."

"So do I," answered Bob, comically.

"When will Herbert be here?" asked Tom, looking at the large *Tribune* clock.

"It's time for him to show up now."

"I should think so, too," replied Tom, with an expression of doubt.

He was thinking about that morning's experience when Herbert failed to appear till after he had breakfasted.

In a little time young Randolph joined them. He was as much surprised as Tom had been at the change made in Bob's personal appearance by his handsome new suit.

"You must go down and let Mr. Goldwin see you with it on," said he.

"When shall we start, Bob?" put in Tom Flannery, who couldn't see the propriety in delaying dinner simply to discuss new clothes.

"Are you so very hungry?" laughed Bob, good naturedly.

"I should think I am, for I haven't had no dinner."

"It don't make no difference, Tom, whether you did or not. You'd be starvin' all the same."

"Well, I can't help it; I think it's time to eat, don't you, Herbert?"

"Yes, it is about time for dinner," replied our hero. "Are you ready to go, Bob?"

"Yes, but we won't go up to the Boss Tweed tonight," replied the young detective, somewhat pompously.

"Bob is goin' to ask us up town for a big lay out," said Tom.

Herbert looked doubtful.

"That's so," said Bob. "We will have kind of a blow out all by ourselves."

"And shall we do the town afterwards, as the bloods say?" asked Tom.

"What does 'doing the town' mean?" asked Herbert. The expression was new to him.

"It's goin' round and seeing the sights," replied Bob. "But come, let's be movin'. We can talk about doin' the town while we are at dinner."

"So I say," said Tom, with characteristic hunger.

CHAPTER XXII.

THE GREAT BANQUET.

"GEWHITTAKER! this is splendid, Bob. I didn't think we was coming to no such tony place as what this is," said Tom Flannery.

"Didn't I tell you it wa'n't no Jim Fisk or Boss Tweed ranch?" replied Bob.

"So you did, Bob; but you see I didn't know about them big glass—what do you call 'em?"

"Chandeliers," suggested Herbert.

"Chandeliers, that's it; but ain't they stunnin', though?"

"Well, there ain't nothin' mean about 'em, I should think," answered Bob.

"No, nor 'bout anything here," said Tom. "I never see so much style slung round before, did you, Herbert?"

"I don't know," answered young Randolph, carelessly.

"Say, Tom, don't make so much fuss about this place. 'Tain't nothin'; no, 'tain't nothin', Tom, beside some er the tony places further up town."

A waiter now came along and handed a bill of fare to Bob, and took away the glasses to fill them with ice.

"Do them fellers always dress up so with a swallow tail on, Bob?" asked Tom.

"Yes, at a swell place, like this is, they do," answered Bob.

"Now that waiter he will be right back and want our orders. The first thing is soup, and there's three kinds—*potage Julienne*, *suprême*, and *consommé à la royale*. Which will you have, Herbert?"

"You may give me the *potage Julienne*," replied the young Vermonter.

"Say 'em again, Bob; I didn't quite catch 'em before," said Tom.

Bob smiled, and obeyed the request.

"Why not have 'em all, Bob?" said Tom, eagerly.

"'Cause 'tain't regular to do that way."

"Well, they are all on there for us, ain't they?"

"They are on for us to take whichever one we want."

"And I can't have but one?"

"No."

"Well, I thought at these er—what do you call 'em?—dinners a feller had everything in the old bill, if he wanted it."

"*Table d'hôte*, you mean, Tom Flannery, but you're way off, you are; nobody ever has everything."

Tom looked disappointed, even sad.

"Well," continued Bob, "I'm waiting for your order. Which soup will you have?"

"Which you goin' to have, Bob?"

"I'm goin' to have the *consommé*."

"Then I'll take the other one," said Tom.

"The *suprême*?"

"That's him," replied Tom.

"Why do you prefer that?" laughed Herbert.

"Well, you see, it sounds better. That one that Bob has took I can't make no sense out of it nohow, and I don't believe it's good to eat, either—anything with a name like that."

THE GREAT BANQUET.

"But the name of your soup is not much better."

"That's so, Herbert. Blamed if I know what they wants to put such stuff on fer a feller to eat fer," said Tom, with an air of disgust.

"Well, Tom, you may as well get used to these names, for you'll get a lot of 'em before you get through this bill," said Bob, laughing.

"Them names don't go all the way through, do they, Bob?" asked Tom, alarmed.

"Yes, plumb through to the end."

"Well, that will spoil my dinner, then, for I don't know nothing about such words."

"No, I guess it won't spoil your dinner, Tom; I'll bet you will eat like a hungry tramp before we get through."

"Maybe I will, Bob Hunter, but I'd like to know what I'm eatin' all the same," replied Tom, somewhat indignant. He did not like to be compared to a hungry tramp.

"That's all right, Tom Flannery; now don't you get off your base so sudden like. You will think you never struck a lay out like this before you get half way down the bill," said Bob, trying to restore good feeling.

"Well, I hope I will, that's what I say. A feller ought to get something good when he has to wade through such blamed old names as these, that don't mean nothin'."

"But they do mean somethin', jest as much as what our words mean to us."

"Do you mean to tell me, Bob Hunter, that anybody uses these words?"

"Of course they do, Tom. They are French words, and French folks know what they mean."

Tom thought for a moment; then he said:

"I was way off, Bob. I thought it was some words jest made up for this bill, 'cause you see I don't know nothin' about French."

The waiter now reappeared, bringing with him two long rolls of French bread, a supply of butter, and three glasses of ice water.

Presently the soup was brought on.

"Sail right in now, Herbert, you and Tom," said Bob. "The next course will be right along."

Tom took a few drops, timidly, then a larger portion—less timidly—and now he put on a full head of steam and worked the spoon like a trip hammer.

When his plate was empty he said: "I think I struck it right, Bob; I knew I hit the best name."

"Why, was yours good, Tom?" replied Bob.

"I should think it was, Bob. It was way up, that's what it was. You see 'tain't always, Bob, that a feller can pick a winner the first time."

"Now you're givin' us some more of your horse racin' expressions, Tom. Can't you never let 'em alone, 'specially at a tony dinner like this is?" said Bob.

"Well, I didn't think about that, Bob. I didn't mean to do nothin' wrong. But you see, Bob, I didn't know of no other way to get at it. This orderin' stuff by these blamed words is takin' chances—what I call bigger chances than bettin' on a horse race."

Young Randolph and Bob laughed heartily at Tom's remarks.

The next course was now put on the table. It came in a large platter. Three plates were placed before Bob, and he served the fish and potatoes in a very creditable manner.

"Now comes the *entrées*," said Bob.

"What are them things, Bob?" said Tom, while ravenously devouring the portion before him.

"Well, I was jest goin' to give 'em to you when you busted in on me," replied Bob. "Here they are:

"*Fillet piqué.*

"*Fricandeau de Veau.*

"*Pâtés aux huitres.*"

"Can't a fellow get more'n one go at 'em, Bob?" said Tom, comically.

"That's all, only one go, Tom; which will you have?"

"I'll take the first one, Bob."

"The *fillet piqué?*"

"Yes, if that's the first one."

"Well, 'tis; but, Tom, you're way off. You didn't pick no winner this time, as you say, for that dish ain't no good."

"Where did you get on to them blamed names, Bob? You're slingin' jest as much style here, too, as you did in the detective business."

"Well, why wouldn't I know 'bout 'em, Tom? Didn't I work in one of these places for a good while, and didn't I pay some attention to the way things was done?"

"So you did, Bob; I didn't think about that."

"I, too, have been surprised, Bob, to see how familiar you seemed with the various dishes," said Herbert.

"Well, that's how it come. You see I picked it up."

"But you are as much at ease serving the dinner as I am at eating it."

"How much?" said Bob, feeling in his pocket for loose change.

"What do you mean?" asked Herbert, seriously.

Bob smiled, and Tom burst into a characteristic laugh. It was the first time since the dinner commenced that he had seen the funny side of anything. Tom Flannery was not given to looking upon the comical side. He was too credulous for that; but when anything did strike him as funny, and he made up his mind to treat it as such, the outburst of laughter that followed—laughter that was rich and childlike—was something to do one good.

Now, there was nothing especially bright or funny about Bob's remark that should have caused Tom to become so hilarious. In fact, it was more Herbert's serious manner, than what Bob said, that set him off.

"'Twas an old chestnut, any way, Bob," as Tom said the next day; "but Herbert looked so honest about it, jest as if you wasn't talkin' jokes, that it jest made me lay myself out and shout. I couldn't er stopped, Bob, ef it had killed me."

When the laughter had subsided, Bob explained his joke to Herbert, and then said:

"You have not told me what you will have. Here comes the waiter for our orders."

"You order 'em, Bob," said Tom. "You know what's good."

"That is a good suggestion, Tom, and meets with my approval," remarked Herbert.

Bob accordingly ordered for all three, and his selection gave excellent satisfaction to his guests.

The next course was simply maccaroni, cooked in the Italian style, with tomato dressing.

"This is bang up, Bob," said Tom Flannery, smacking his lips. "Them Eyetalians are some good after all, ain't they?"

Roast duck followed the maccaroni, with jelly, and fine cut celery with dressing.

Then came ice cream, followed by cheese—*fromage de Brie.*

"Bob, there's somethin' wrong about this," said Tom, seriously, referring to the last course. "Jest get on to that piece, will you?" and Tom passed his portion to Bob.

"Don't be a fool, now, Tom Flannery," said Bob, with assumed displeasure, while he struggled hard to keep from giggling.

"Well, I ain't no fool, Bob; I guess I know when I know a thing," said Tom, indignantly. "I tell you that piece is all spoilt," and, to make sure of his statement, he took it in his fingers, and without regard to good manners placed it close to his nose, and gave it a genuine test.

Bob threw himself back in the chair, and exploded with laughter. Herbert did likewise. But Tom was mad. He thought Bob had played a trick on him, and he said:

"I don't intend to be imposed upon in any such way as what this is, Bob Hunter. I'll show you that I can put up jobs, too, ef you think it is so much fun."

Now Brie cheese is somewhat soft, so much so that it many times adheres slightly to whatever it touches. Tom had rashly taken it up in his fingers, and now, while breathing forth malice and threats against Bob, he chanced to put his fingers up to his mouth. This brought them again in close proximity to his nose.

"Gewhopper!" yelled Tom, as he thrust his hand into his trousers pocket with a view to better protecting his nose. "I wouldn't er thought this of you, Bob Hunter!"

Both Bob and Herbert were convulsed with laughter, and were holding their sides from pain.

From the fact that they laughed so uncontrollably, and that they did not deny his charge, Tom felt sure that he had been made the butt of a foul joke, and he resented it spunkily. This of course only made the situation more ridiculous, and the more Tom said, the harder Bob and Herbert laughed. At length, however, Bob quieted down sufficiently to remark:

"Tom, listen to me. You're the biggest fool I ever see."

"Yes, you think you've made a fool of me, don't you, Bob Hunter? But you hain't, for I got on to your game before I got any er that durned stuff into my mouth."

"Oh, don't you be so ignorant, Tom Flannery. The trouble is with you, you're a chump, you don't know nothin' about livin' at high toned places like this is."

"No, nor I don't want to nuther, Bob Hunter. Ef that stuff is what you call high toned livin', why I don't want no more of it in mine. I'll——"

In the excitement of the conversation, Tom forgot to keep his hand housed up longer in his pocket, and now the tips of his fingers unconsciously found their way close to his nose again.

This was what caused Tom to break off his sentence so abruptly. He didn't say anything for a minute, but he looked a whole volume of epithets.

Herbert and Bob started in on another round of laughter that still further irritated Tom.

"I'm goin'," said he, slinging his napkin savagely upon the table; "I won't stand this business no more, Bob Hunter."

"Sit down, Tom," commanded Bob; "there's more to come yet. You hain't had no coffee yet, nor nuts and raisins."

Tom immediately replaced the napkin in his lap, and pulled up to the table again. Coffee, nuts and raisins! Oh, no, Tom

Flannery couldn't allow his grievance to deprive him of these luxuries!

"Now, Tom," said Bob, "I jest want to show you that you've made a fool of yourself, and that we hain't made no fool of you. Of course we couldn't help laughin' to see you actin' so redikerlus, Tom, and all about a little piece of cheese, too. A feller would er thought, Tom, that you'd been dumped in a sewer, to see you carry on; but when you get one er them crazy notions in your head, why, there's no doin' anything with you, but to let you sail in and enjoy yourself."

Bob then ate his choice bit of Brie with a keen relish, much to the surprise of Tom, and I may say Herbert as well, for the latter's taste had not been educated up to the point where he could eat such food.

At length reconciliation was reached, and Tom was once more happy. When the coffee had been drunk, the three boys, while eating nuts and raisins, discussed the problem of money making.

"How about the Wall Street racket?" remarked Tom.

"You refer to speculating, I suppose?" replied Herbert.

"Yes. You see my capital ain't earnin' me nothin'."

"Well, I have had very little time to think about that since we first spoke of it. In fact, I am not in favor of the idea."

"What! not in favor of spekerlatin'?" said Bob, with astonishment.

"Nuther am I," put in Tom, wisely; "I don't think it's safe."

"But you think it's safe to bet on horse racin', don't you, Tom Flannery?"

"Well, it's safer'n what spekerlatin' is, that's what I think, Bob Hunter."

"Humph! You know a lot, don't you, Tom Flannery?"

"No, I don't know a lot about them Wall Street schemes, ef that's what you mean; but I guess I can pick a winner at racin'."

"Well, ef you don't know nothin' about spekerlatin', how are you goin' to use any judgment? Tell me that now, Tom Flannery."

"You kinder want to bulldoze me, don't you, Bob Hunter? You've got your head sot on spekerlatin', and you want to make me think jest like you do."

"You tire me, Tom Flannery," said Bob, with a great show of disgust. "I'd try and have some sense, ef I was you."

"All right, Bob, then I'll try 'n' have some sense—I'll do jest as you say, and spekerlate till my five dollars is all blowed in. Now, does that satisfy you, Bob?"

Tom Flannery had almost always yielded readily to Bob's judgment. This sudden independence of opinion, therefore, was a surprise to young Hunter.

"Why, that's all right, Tom," said he, instantly changing his attitude. "I don't care nothin' about your spekerlatin' ef you don't want to; but I want to make some money, that's what I do, and I thought you did too, Tom."

"So I do, Bob, so I do; but you see so many folks loses money down there in Wall Street, and some of them big fellers, too, with heaps of money, just dead loads of it, to back 'em."

"Well, that's so, Tom, I know they loses sometimes, but don't lots of 'em make money? Now answer me that."

"Yes, you are right, Bob, they do some of 'em strike it rich, but as you said about the racin' I guess the money ain't good money, fer it don't stick to 'em."

"Well, I should think it stuck to Jay Gould, didn't it?"

"Yes, he is one of the few successful ones," said Herbert, answering the question for Tom.

"Yes, but there are lots and lots of them kings of Wall Street," persisted Bob, who had a strong desire to become a speculator.

"So there are, Bob," replied Herbert, "but they do not hold their rank throughout their lives. A man that is called a king in Wall Street one day, may be a beggar the next day."

"Think of that, Bob," put in Tom Flannery, exultantly.

"Well, I know, but then them kings don't all go up like that."

"But the majority of them do. If you will get a book that gives the history of Wall Street, you will be surprised to see how thousands, hundreds of thousands, and even millions, are swept away almost without warning."

"Whew! just think of it! A whole million dollars!" exclaimed Tom. "Say, Herbert, how much is a million dollars? It must be a whoppin' big pile, that's what I think."

"A million dollars—let me see, Tom, how I can explain it so that you will comprehend its——"

"So I will what?" interrupted Tom, doubtful of the meaning of the word "comprehend."

Herbert made this clear, and then said:

"Now, Tom, you have a five dollar bill, and——"

"Yes, and it's a new one, too, crisp as a ginger snap," interrupted young Flannery.

"All right, then, a new five dollar bill. Now, suppose you had altogether twenty bills just like this one, you would have how much money?"

"Can you tell, Bob?" said Tom, grinning.

"Why, of course I can!" replied Bob, throwing his head back, proudly.

"Well, let's see ef you can."

"One hundred dollars," answered Bob.

"I guess that's right, Herbert, a hundred dollars; but I never see so much money all at one time, did you, Bob?"

Herbert proceeded with the illustration by saying:

"Then, Tom, you understand how many five dollar bills it takes to make one hundred dollars. Now, it would require ten one hundred dollar bills to make one one thousand dollar bill."

"Gewhopple! that's climbin' up, ain't it, Bob?" exclaimed Tom, incredulously.

"Oh, but that's nothing," said Herbert. "Just listen: It would take a hundred one thousand dollar bills to make one hundred thousand dollars, and it would require ten times one hundred thousand dollars to make one million."

"Well, that's fur enough," said Tom, scratching his head. "Don't give me no more tonight, for I can't take it in no way. A million dollars; and you say some er them kings loses so much money as all this in almost no time?"

"Why, yes; perhaps in a single day," answered Herbert.

"And you think, Bob Hunter, that we could go down there with only five dollars apiece and lay out them kings and scoop the boodle, do you? Now, answer me that."

"Well, it does seem kinder like takin' chances, ef them fellers loses money like that."

"Of course it does, Bob, fer you see we wouldn't have but one go at the game with only five dollars; would we, Herbert?"

"Five dollars wouldn't go very far, for a fact," replied Herbert, "and in my opinion it would be lost very quickly."

"But I've heard of fellers that went down there without no money, and they made loads of it."

"Very true," said Herbert; "but did you ever hear of the thousands that went down there and came away without a cent?"

"No, I never did," admitted Bob, frankly.

Tom smiled quietly, for he felt that Bob would have to acknowledge himself mistaken, and at last come over to his side.

"Well, now, there is the very point," said Herbert, "and it is the one that nobody stops to think about. A report is circulated that some one makes a big haul in Wall Street, and, without thinking about the thousands of people that lose money there, a thousand or two more people try their luck at speculating, thinking, each one of them, to make a great haul too. But the result is the same as it was with the other thousand speculators—the money is swallowed up, and gone forever."

"What becomes of it all?" asked Bob, much impressed by Herbert's well founded argument.

"Well, the most of it goes into the pockets of the kings."

"Then I shouldn't think them kings would get busted, as you say they do," said Bob, always keen at making a point.

"They would not if they had to deal only with the small speculators, such as you would like to be. If that were the case they would win nearly every time. But kings are the ones who break kings."

"Oh, I see now," said Bob. "There are a lot of 'em, and they jest go for each other. Is that it?"

"Yes, that is the way they do it."

"Well, I guess you are right, then, Herbert—you and Tom."

"I feel sure I am. Mr. Goldwin talked with me about it today, and told me never to speculate."

"But he speculates," said Bob, "and he is worth a lot of money."

"Oh, no, never."

"What's he call himself a broker for, then?"

"Why, a broker is not necessarily a speculator. A broker is one who buys and sells stocks or bonds for some one else—for a speculator, and he gets his commission or pay for doing the business."

"Well, I guess I was way off, Herbert. I thought all of them brokers was speculators, and I knew lots of 'em was solid with money."

"Yes, that is the way of it," replied Herbert. "The broker makes the money and the speculator loses it, usually."

"Don't brokers never lose nothin', Herbert?" asked Tom.

"No, not unless they trust some one who fails to pay them."

"Well, I thought you would get sick er spekerlatin', Bob, and I'm glad you've done it before you're broke," said Tom Flannery. "I don't want no spekerlatin' for me."

"No, but you'd like a go at horse racin' all the same, Tom Flannery," said Bob.

"No, I wouldn't nuther, Bob, fer you talked me out er bettin' and into spekerlatin', and now Herbert here has jest upset the spekerlatin' idea, so I'm out of it all, Bob."

"Good," said Herbert; "I am glad you have come to so wise a decision."

"So am I," said Bob, heartily.

"So am I," echoed Tom, with equal fervor.

"But now," said Bob, "what are we goin' to do with our money? It ain't earnin' us nothin', you see."

"I think the best plan, Bob," said Herbert, thoughtfully, "would be for you and Tom to put your money in the savings bank. There it will be safe, and will be earning a little interest all the time. Let it remain there until we see a chance to invest it to good advantage, and in the meantime add as much to it as possible."

"I never thought of that before," said Bob.

"Nuther did I," added Tom.

"Strikes me 'tain't a bad scheme," continued Bob. "What do you say, Tom?"

"Well, I don't see no great money in it, anyhow," answered young Flannery. "But if Herbert says it's the best thing, why I s'pose 'tis."

"It is the best plan, I am sure," said young Randolph. "Very few speculators ever come out rich. The men who gain wealth are those who invest their money carefully, and put it where it will be safe."

CHAPTER XXIII.

BOB HUNTER'S AMBITION.

ON the following day, after the paper trade of the morning was over, Bob and Tom, acting upon young Randolph's advice, went to the Emigrants' Industrial Savings Bank, and deposited each five dollars. They felt very proud as they came out into Chambers Street with their bank books.

"It's a starter any way," said Bob.

"I've been thinking over what Herbert said, and I guess between you'n me, Tom, he is 'bout right."

"That's what I think too, Bob," replied young Flannery, for aside from the matter of betting on horse racing and speculating, he always agreed with Bob.

"I think we was in big luck, Tom, when we run on to Herbert Randolph."

"I think so, too, Bob; but why do you think so?"

"Why do I think so! Well, ef that ain't a queer question, Tom Flannery. Would you a' had that bank book now, with your name, Thomas Flannery, in plain writin' writ across it, I'd like to know, ef it hadn't been for Vermont?"

"No, I wouldn't. That's so, Bob, I wouldn't, fer to be honest with you, Bob, I think I'd put it on racin'."

"So you would, Tom, ef you'd had it, but you wouldn't er had it."

"Well, I never thought of that, Bob, but it's so, ain't it?"

"I should say it is, and I wouldn'ter had my bank book or these new clothes either."

"And the big supper, Bob?"

"That's so, Tom, and the big supper too. I tell you, Tom Flannery, 'twas great luck when we struck Vermont."

"That's so, Bob, so it was. But say, Bob, don't you think 'twas kinder lucky for Herbert when he fell in with you?"

BOB AND TOM COMING OUT OF THE BANK.

"I don't know 'bout that, Tom. How do you figure it?"

"Why, I figures it in this way, Bob; ef it hadn't been fer you he would be down in that old Gunwagner's cellar now."

"Well, that's so, Tom, but he has more than paid me up, though."

"How did he do it, Bob?" asked Tom eagerly.

"Ain't he helping me right along, I'd like to know?"

"I hain't heard much about it, Bob. What has he done for you?"

"Yes, you have heard about it, too, Tom Flannery. Didn't I tell you how he teaches me every night?"

"Oh, yes, you told me about that, Bob, but that ain't much—'tain't like doin' the detective business, is it?"

"Well, no, of course it hain't, but it's just as good, Tom, and a good deal more so, I think."

"Well, I don't think no such thing, Bob."

"Well, ef I do, that's all right, ain't it? I tell you, Tom, 'tain't every feller that can do the teachin' act."

"Nuther can every fellow do the detective business. Ef you want to know what I think, Bob Hunter, I'll tell you."

"All right, Tom, sail in."

"Well, I think, ef I was you, I'd jest let this learnin' business go, and I'd make myself a detective. No feller could put more style into it than what you could, Bob."

"Tom, you're way off again. A feller can't make no kind of a detective, nor nothin' else, neither, unless he knows somethin'. I guess I know, and Herbert says so too."

"Well, I hain't got no learnin'," replied Tom, somewhat pompously, as if to prove by himself that Bob's statement was untrue.

"I know it," said Bob, and stopped short.

Tom looked at him doubtfully.

"Then you might's well say right out that I won't make nothin', Bob Hunter," said he, his manner resembling that of one not a little indignant.

"Well, I said what I said, Tom, and if it fits you, why then am I to blame?"

Tom made no reply.

"It's no use for you to get mad, Tom. Anybody would tell you jest the same as what I did. Now, the thing for you to do, Tom, is ter get some learnin'—you can do it."

"Do you think I could, Bob?" replied Tom, coming round to Bob's views, as he almost always did.

"Why, of course you could, Tom; ain't I doin' it?"

"Well, yes, I s'pose you are, Bob, but then you can do 'most anything."

"That ain't so, Tom. You can do it jest as well as what I can, ef you only try."

"I never thought about that before, Bob," said Tom, thoughtfully. "Who could I get to learn me?"

"You mustn't say 'learn you,' Tom. Herbert says that hain't right."

"What is it, then, Bob?"

"He says I must say 'teach me,' because I've got to do the learning myself."

"Well, that's too much for me, Bob; I want to start in on somethin' easier."

At length this discussion ended by Tom falling in with Bob's opinion as usual, and by his agreeing to commence at once attending an evening school.

CHAPTER XXIV.

A VISIT TO THE BANKER'S HOUSE.

THE disturbing elements that had produced the somewhat dramatic and extraordinary scenes of the last week were now apparently quiet. But were they actually so? This is the question that Herbert Randolph and Bob Hunter asked themselves—a question that caused them much anxiety.

Felix Mortimer, to be sure, was in the Tombs awaiting his trial. But the granite wall and the great iron doors were alike powerless to imprison his mind. He was as free as ever to think and to plot. What schemes of revenge might not then be planned by this boy whose hatred for Herbert Randolph now undoubtedly burned more fiercely than ever? And Gunwagner, his companion in crime, was free to carry out any plan that might be agreed upon between them. He had given bonds to appear when wanted by the court, something that Felix Mortimer was unable to do. This is why the latter was still locked up, while the old fence was allowed his temporary freedom.

Except for the constant anxiety that Herbert and Bob felt over this matter, everything went smoothly with them. Papers sold briskly, work at the bank was congenial, and they had already become much interested in each other. The days flew by quickly, and they looked forward to the evenings, which they spent together as a time for enjoyment and improvement. As often as Tom Flannery could leave his evening school he joined them, and he was always welcome. No one could help liking him, he was so simple and honest. How keenly he enjoyed an evening with Herbert and Bob in their room, or strolling about the great city, as they not infrequently did! Their slender means would not warrant them in attending the theater often. Occasionally, however, they managed to get inexpensive admission tickets to a really good play. Bob Hunter usually procured them as a reward for some service he had given during the day, when his paper trade did not demand his attention. Many very good free lectures, too, were open to them, and they seldom failed to improve this opportunity. The Young Men's Christian Association building, with its fine library and gymnasium, proved a very attractive resort to these three boys, whose happiness, though they lived in the most humble way, was doubtless equaled by few boys in the great metropolis, however luxurious their home and surroundings.

One evening in particular young Randolph found especially enjoyable. It came about in this way. Mr. Goldwin had a slight attack of rheumatism that caused him to remain at home. He sent a note to his office saying he should not be at the bank on that day, and requesting Herbert to come to his house late in the afternoon, and to bring with him a report of the day's business, and whatever mail it would be desirable for the banker to see.

The young Vermonter read the note eagerly, and then immediately did the same thing over again. A peculiar pleasure shone in his eyes as he looked doubtingly at the little piece of paper. And now he saw a very attractive picture—a rich family carriage into which a charmingly pretty girl was being helped by a blushing boy. He wondered why she had never been at the bank since that time, and speculated dreamily upon his chance of seeing her at her father's house.

Thus the day wore away, and at the close of business hours young Randolph hurried from the bank, taking with him what he had been requested to bring.

At City Hall Park he stopped and informed Bob Hunter of his mission, and then went quickly to his room to put himself into the most presentable appearance possible with the somewhat scanty resources of his wardrobe.

His heart beat fast with expectations and fears as he ascended the brown stone steps of Mr. Goldwin's house.

"Good evening, Mr. Randolph," said the banker, greeting Herbert very cordially. "I hope you have a good report of today's transactions for me."

"Yes, I think this statement of the transactions will please you," replied young Randolph politely.

"Excellent," exclaimed the banker with a smile of satisfaction, as he read the report. "You have done a splendid day's work. The market must have been unusually active. Why, here is a transaction of twenty thousand shares by one house alone—great customers, Breakwell & Co., great customers, bold men—not afraid of anything."

"They certainly seem to be very enterprising," remarked Herbert, feeling the necessity of saying something, and that that something should concur with his employer's views.

"Most assuredly they are," answered the banker, warming to the subject. "Why, if we had more houses like Breakwell & Co., Wall Street would see no dull days—no, sir, none at all. On the contrary, it would just hum with activity."

"I suppose they are perfectly good, Mr. Goldwin," remarked Herbert, not knowing what better reply to make.

"Good? Why, they are rated A1, and are reported to be very rich," replied the banker.

HERBERT'S FIRST VISIT TO THE BANKER'S HOUSE.

"Did they make their money by speculating?"

"Yes, I understand so."

"Are they sure of keeping it if they continue to speculate?"

"Well, now, you are asking me a difficult question. Nothing, you know, is certain in Wall Street."

Before Herbert had time to reply, dinner was announced. The question touching the reliability of Breakwell & Co. was immediately dropped, and in its place arose the unexpected problem whether or not he should accept the banker's invitation to dine with him and his family. He would have quite as soon thought of receiving an invitation to dinner from the mayor himself. It was quite natural, therefore, that he should offer some ridiculous reason why he should be excused, when, as a matter of fact, he would have much rather served another term of imprisonment at old Gunwagner's than lose this opportunity.

"Come right along," commanded Mr. Goldwin, himself leading the way.

Herbert followed the banker into the parlor, where he was introduced to his employer's wife and daughter.

He found himself blushing even more profusely than when he had handed Ray Goldwin into her carriage, at the close of his first day's service for her father. This heightened color, too, seemed to be reflected upon her cheeks, and her manner indicated a slight but not unnatural embarrassment.

Herbert had thought that the dinner given by Bob Hunter was about as good as could well be served, but this one proved in every respect much the better; and notwithstanding his nervousness and lack of ease, under circumstances so unfamiliar, he enjoyed the meal greatly.

While Herbert Randolph could laugh at the drollery and peculiar street language of Bob Hunter and Tom Flannery, he nevertheless found a higher degree of pleasure in the conversation of this intelligent and refined family.

"Papa told us about your imprisonment, Mr. Randolph," said Ray, looking wonderfully pretty, as Herbert thought. "It must have been dreadful."

"It was an unpleasant experience," replied young Randolph, lightly; "but I came out all right."

"Ah, that reminds me," said Mr. Goldwin, "that one of the letters you brought me was from my attorney. In it he expressed the opinion that you can recover damages from the old fence for false imprisonment. I would therefore advise you to place the matter in his hands at once, and have him push it."

"You mean put it into the hands of your lawyer?"

"YOU EMBARRASS ME," SAID HERBERT, BLUSHING.

"Yes."

"I appreciate very highly your interest in my behalf, Mr. Goldwin, and I will do as you say," replied Herbert.

"Wouldn't it be splendid if you could get damages from that dreadful old man?" said Ray, with enthusiasm.

Thus the conversation ran on, and before the dinner had been finished, Herbert felt himself quite well acquainted with both Mrs. Goldwin and Ray. He had tried to convince himself that he did not care for girls, and he thought he had succeeded well in doing so. But for some inexplicable reason, his imaginary objections to the sex in general did not stand long against Ray Goldwin in particular.

Her bright blue eyes, brimful of spirit and laughter, seemed to detect his aversion, and she aimed, he thought, to show him that he had deceived himself.

After the meal had been finished all repaired to the library, where, after a half hour of social converse, Herbert wrote several letters for Mr. Goldwin at his dictation. Ray sat opposite him with the purpose of reading, but as a matter of fact she did not progress very fast with the story.

"Would you be willing to write in my autograph album, Mr. Randolph?" said she, somewhat timidly, when he had finished her father's letters.

"Yes, I will do so with pleasure," he answered.

"I shall be proud of such pretty writing," returned Ray, handing him the book.

"You embarrass me," said he, blushing.

"I don't see why," laughed Ray, enjoying young Randolph's modesty.

"Well, I am not accustomed to compliments, especially from—er——"

"From young girls," suggested Mrs. Goldwin, smiling.

"Thank you," returned Herbert; "I was hesitating whether to say 'girls' or 'young ladies.'"

"Oh, say girls, by all means," replied Mrs. Goldwin. "We don't want Ray to become a young lady too soon."

"I don't blame you," responded our hero, half seriously.

"Why, Mr. Randolph," said Ray, shaking her dainty finger at him. "I believe I would not have asked you to write in my album if I had supposed you would say that."

"Well, it is not too late yet, for you see I have not touched the book with the pen," laughed Herbert.

"Oh, but I would not want to disappoint you. You know you said it would give you pleasure to do so."

"So it would, but I would rather sacrifice this pleasure than feel that you would be sorry you had given me the invitation."

Without further parley Herbert wrote in the album—wrote so prettily that he was roundly complimented by all.

Mrs. Goldwin and Ray were now summoned into the drawing room to receive a caller, and presently young Randolph took his leave, and started for his room with a very light and happy heart.

CHAPTER XXV.

TOM FLANNERY'S SICKNESS.

BOB HUNTER was too much surprised by the fact that Herbert was going to Mr. Goldwin's house to tell him of his own anxiety about Tom Flannery. The latter had not, as Bob learned, been seen for two days at his accustomed place. That he should be away one day was not particularly strange, for he not infrequently got odd jobs to do that took him to another part of the city, or possibly to some of the near by suburbs. Two days' absence, however, was so unusual for him that Bob Hunter became anxious, fearing that possibly the vengeance of old Gunwagner and his companion in crime had fallen upon poor, unsuspecting Tom. This thought having suggested itself to him, his previous anxiety speedily turned to a feeling of alarm.

He therefore left his place of business as early as possible, and after a hurried supper went quickly to Tom Flannery's home, which was in a large office building on Broadway, very near Bowling Green. The latter's mother was janitress of the building. Her duties were to keep it clean, and to look after the interests of the owner. For these services she received a trifling money reward, and was allowed to occupy two small rooms at the top of the building. Here Mrs. Flannery and Tom made their home, which, though humble, was very neat.

Bob knocked softly at the door, out of breath from climbing so many flights of stairs, and with sore misgivings for the safety of his young companion. The door was opened presently by a woman of middle age, who, as Bob saw at a glance from her extraordinary resemblance to Tom, was the newsboy's mother. He had never seen her before, but the honest, trustful look so characteristic of his young friend shone prominently in Mrs. Flannery's face.

"They have got him, poor Tom," said Bob to himself with beating heart, as he saw Mrs. Flannery's grief.

"Are you not Master Bob Hunter?" said the woman, speaking first—after an awkward pause; for the visitor, who had been so bold a detective, was now so distressed that he knew not what to say.

"Yes, I am Bob Hunter," was the soft reply.

"And you are come to see my boy—my poor Tom?" said the woman, pressing Bob's hand warmly, and struggling vainly to keep back the tears.

"Is he here?" asked Bob, dumfounded by the contradictory state of things; for it was apparent from the woman's question that Tom was at home, and, he being at home, why such grief?

"I'm so glad you came to see him, for he thought so much of you, Master Bob," said Mrs. Flannery, now giving way entirely to her feelings.

"I would have come before if I had known——"

"I know you would, I know you would," interrupted the woman between sobs, "and he asked so many times for you, and now to think that you are here and he won't know you. Oh, my poor Tom!"

"I don't blame you for being proud, Bob. I wish I had

such a case too, but then I couldn't handle it not the way you could, Bob. None of the fellers could, not one of 'em, Bob, for you do everything in such a grand way, you know."

These words, so familiar yet so ominously strange, fell upon Bob Hunter like a messenger of death.

"Oh, what is it, Mrs. Flannery? What has happened to Tom?" cried he, pale with fright.

"It's his head, Master Bob—gone since morning—rambling on just like this—detectives, and I don't know what all."

"Have you had a doctor to see him?" asked Bob, his mind turning quickly to practical measures.

"Yes, and he says it's pneumonia, and a very bad case," answered the mother, with almost a hopeless expression.

Bob learned that Tom came home two days before thoroughly wet from a cold northeast rain; that he had a chill soon after going to bed; that he grew rapidly worse throughout the night, and that in the morning he had a high fever. Mrs. Flannery called in a doctor, who, after a careful examination, pronounced the case pneumonia. He left medicine which seemed to afford temporary relief. In the night, however, Tom grew worse, and during the following forenoon became delirious.

"Don't you know me, Tom?" said Bob feelingly, as he stood by the bedside, and held the sufferer's hand in his own.

"All the evening papers—*Sun, Mail and Express, Telegram*—big accident—tremendous loss of life! Which will you have, sir?"

And this was Tom's wild reply, poor boy. Now that his companion, whom he wanted to see so much, and for whom he had such admiration, had at last come to him, the sick boy did not know him; but supposing he had a customer for his papers, he rattled on in true newsboy fashion. Bob tried again and again to rouse his mind by referring to Herbert Randolph, and to scenes familiar and interesting, but his efforts were unsuccessful. At length his stout young heart gave way, and with an expression of the keenest grief he dropped into a chair beside the bed, burying his face in the pure white spread that covered his young companion, and wept tears of sincere sorrow.

TOM FLANNERY IN DELIRIUM.

Presently he withdrew from the sick room, and after a brief discussion with Mrs. Flannery hurried away to the doctor whom she had previously called in to see Tom. The physician promised to visit the sick boy again within an hour. Having this assurance from the doctor, Bob then turned his steps towards his own room to acquaint Herbert Randolph with Tom's illness. But to Bob's surprise he found on arriving there that the young Vermonter had not yet reached home.

"'Twas nine o'clock when I passed the *Tribune* building," said Bob to himself rather anxiously, "and he hain't come yet.

I hope nothing's gone bad with him, though, for we've got trouble enough on our hands already, with Tom sick, and goin' to die, I'm afraid. I wish I could do something for him; he would do anything in the world for me, Tom would."

But Bob's fears regarding Herbert proved groundless, for in a little time the latter joined him with a light heart, made happy by the very kind reception given him at Mr. Goldwin's.

On his way home his mind was filled with the vision of a sweet young face, which to him was an inspiration. And as he hurried along the avenue, thinking faster and faster, what charming pictures his imagination brought before him—pictures that for him possessed a strange and peculiar attraction. But these beautiful creations of his mind were quickly lost to him when he saw the troubled look on young Bob Hunter's face.

"Why, Bob," said he, "what makes you look so wretched? What has happened?"

The latter quickly related the story of Tom's sickness, and stated his own fears.

"I cannot realize it, Bob," said Herbert, deeply touched. "Poor Tom! let us go at once and do whatever we can for him."

"That's right, Herbert; that's what I think we ought to do, and I shouldn't come home at all only I knew you would not know what had become of me," replied Bob, as they put on their overcoats and started for Mrs. Flannery's humble home.

CHAPTER XXVI.

A CRASH IN WALL STREET.

AT the end of two weeks Tom was again up and dressed. His struggle with the pneumonia had been a frightful one. It was turned in his favor largely by the aid of the best medical skill, and the untiring care given him by his mother and his two faithful friends, Herbert and Bob. The latter took turns in watching with him at night, while Mrs. Flannery slept, that she might renew her strength for the day watch.

But the disease, as is not infrequently the case, left Tom with a hard, dry cough, which threatened serious results. His lungs were weak, and his body was much emaciated. He was not the Tom Flannery of old, the Tom so full of boyish spirits and desire to push his paper trade. This change in their young companion caused Herbert and Bob keen anxiety. They had watched beside his bed through delirium and helplessness, when there seemed no hope of his recovery. How glad their young hearts were when he began to rally, and they could see him in imagination back with them again in their old pleasures and pastimes! His failure, therefore, to throw off the racking cough and regain his strength was a sore disappointment to them, but this was not their only source of apprehension.

How full these two weeks had been of bitter trouble—trouble

that drew deeply upon their sympathy; that destroyed splendid prospects and forced one of them from a position of independence to one little better than beggary.

Disturbing elements had been gathering for days in Wall Street, which to a few wise old heads seemed ominous. They predicted danger, but their warnings were laughed at by the less cautious speculators, who operated with a reckless daring. At length, however, the storm struck almost without a moment's notice. Wild reports filled the air, and men, strong, bold men, crushed by the tremendous force of the panic, fell prostrate here and there, and everywhere Terror spread to all, and painted its sickly hue upon their faces. When the storm had subsided the street was full of wrecks. Among them was the daring firm of Breakwell & Co., who had failed for a million and a quarter of dollars.

Young Randolph was stunned at the exhibition he witnessed on that fatal day. House after house with whom his firm had done business, and who were supposed to be almost beyond the possibility of failure, had closed their doors. Breakwell & Co. were among the last to go under. They had been kept up by the splendid loyalty of Richard Goldwin, who put his bank account at their command, relying upon their assurance that they were all right, and would come out of the storm stronger than ever, if they could only receive temporary help. Mr. Goldwin, anxious to save them, stood heroically by them, and went down with them—a victim of noble generosity, of misplaced confidence. Yes, he had failed—Richard Goldwin, the banker and broker, yesterday a millionaire, today perhaps a pauper.

Herbert Randolph could not at first realize the awful fact, but the pain he saw in Mr. Goldwin's face appealed so strongly to his sympathy that the tears forced themselves from his eyes, try however bravely he would to restrain them. The doors were closed, and all business with the house of Richard Goldwin was at an end.

Mr. Goldwin bore the misfortune like a hero. His face was white and firm as marble. Certain lines, however, told his distress, but never a word of complaint at the miserable treachery of Breakwell & Co. escaped his lips.

Herbert could not help thinking how severe the shock would be to Mrs. Goldwin and Ray, who could not bridle their emotions with an iron will like that of the ruined banker. The latter was accustomed, in his long career in Wall Street, to seeing others meet the disaster that had now overtaken him; but his wife and daughter—ah, how little they were prepared for such a shock.

The panic that ruined so many men added quite largely to the fortunes of young Bob Hunter. He had never before had such a trade. Papers sold beyond all imagination, and at double their usual price. The result was a profit of seven dollars and forty seven cents for his day's work. He felt richer than ever before in his life, and so happy that he could hardly wait till the usual time for Herbert to join him, he wanted so much to make known his grand success. But when young Randolph came to him with the sad story of that day in Wall Street, his happiness gave place to a feeling of unusual sadness, and the sadness deepened on learning that his friend was now out of a position.

"But you can get another place, Herbert," said he, reassuringly; "perhaps a better one than you have lost."

"I hope so," was all the reply the young bank clerk made, but there was a world of expression in the way he said it. His face, too, looked the disappointment and sorrow he felt, and

Bob rightly divined that the sorrow was more for Mr. Goldwin and his family than for himself.

It is safe to presume that Herbert thought long and regretfully of the probability of Mr. Goldwin being reduced to a state of poverty—of his being turned out of his luxurious home—of Ray, his daughter, being obliged to work for her living—of her young, sweet life being embittered by want and miserable surroundings, so out of keeping with her beauty and genial, sunny nature. And if he did think in this wise, what resolutions he formed for relieving her of such a life, and of restoring her to her proper place we can only imagine, for on this matter he said never a word, not even to Bob Hunter.

On the following morning, Bob Hunter handed Herbert a small roll of bills.

"What is this for?" said the latter.

"It's for you," replied Bob. "There's only eight dollars in it, but you'll perhaps need it, and then you'll feel better with it in your pocket while looking for work."

"But I cannot accept your money, Bob," protested Herbert, with feelings of deep gratitude.

"Yes, you must, for you are out in the cold, and my business is good; and then, you know, I made 'most all of it yesterday out of the failures in Wall Street—out of your firm's failure as much as any, probably, and that meant your failure to keep your place; so in a way I kinder made it out of you, and now I want you to have it again."

Herbert's eyes were now moist.

"Bob, you are very good and generous," said he, rather huskily; "but you are not logical. I have no claim on your money, neither has any one. You made it in legitimate trade, and should not feel that it does not belong to you."

YOUNG RANDOLPH AGAIN IN THE RANKS OF THE UNEMPLOYED.

"Well, I know I did; but I feel in a kind of way that it was made off of the misfortunes of others, you see."

"But the misfortunes were not caused by you. They had occurred, and people wanted to know about them, and were willing and glad to pay for their information. This gave you an opportunity to make some money, and you made it."

"Well, of course you will beat me at arguing, Herbert, for you always do; but all the same I wish you would take the money, for I think you will need it."

"If I do need any money, when mine is gone, I will then borrow this of you, but until then you must keep it."

After this discussion, and after a very frugal breakfast, Herbert once more joined the ranks of the vast army who go from place to place, hungry and thinly clothed many times, in search of employment—anything to keep the wolf from the door.

CHAPTER XXVII.

DARK DAYS.

IT was now midwinter. The streets were filled with snow and ice, and the cold, frost laden air was chilling alike to the body and spirits of one in the unfortunate position in which young Randolph suddenly found himself.

If one has never been out of a position in a great city at this season of the year, he can have but little conception of the almost utterly hopeless prospects before him. After the holiday trade is over, a vast number of clerks are discharged from our stores, and thousands in the manufacturing line are thrown out of employment. These are added to the very large number that at all seasons of the year are hunting for work. Thousands, too, from the country, thinking to escape the dreary frost bound months of rural life, flock to the city and join the enormous army of the unemployed. All want work, and there is little or no work to be had. It is the season of the year when few changes are made by employers other than to dispense with the services of those not actually needed. To be sure, a few employees die, and leave vacancies to be filled. Others prove unfaithful, and are discharged. A new business, too, is started here and there, but all the available positions combined are as nothing when compared to the tremendous demand for them by the thousands of applicants.

When Herbert Randolph came to New York in the fall,

he was fortunate in arriving at the time when employers usually carry a larger force of help than at any other season of the year. There was consequently less demand for positions, and a greater demand for help. Thus he had a possible chance of securing employment, and he happened to be fortunate enough to do so. I say he had a *possible chance*, for surely he had no more than that even at the most favorable season of the year. He was extremely fortunate, coming from the country as he did, to find employment at all.

In view of these facts it will not be surprising that young Randolph, brave boy as he was, looked upon the dreary prospect before him with a heavy heart.

Bob Hunter realized fully the gravity of his friend's situation, and this is why he urged the money upon him, wishing to keep up his courage, and delicately refraining from touching upon the dark outlook ahead.

I wish I had the space to picture carefully all the rebuffs, the cold treatment, and the discouragement that met our young hero on his daily wanderings, seeking for some honest labor—anything that would furnish him with the means to buy bread. But as I should not feel justified in extending this story to such a length, I must content myself with a few glimpses that will show the heroic struggle he made to sustain himself during these dark, chilly, and cheerless days of winter.

"It's pretty tough, ain't it, Herbert?" said Bob, one night when they were alone together in their room. He sought to lift the burden from his friend's mind by drawing him into conversation.

"Yes," answered Herbert, mechanically.

This reply, so short, and given with so little expression, gave Bob a feeling of uneasiness.

"I hope you ain't getting discouraged," he ventured next.

"No, nothing will discourage me now," replied young Randolph doggedly.

"But you hain't got no encouragement yet?"

"No, none whatever," was the gloomy answer.

"And you've been trying for three weeks to strike something?"

"Yes; it's nearer four weeks, and my shoes are worn out with walking."

"But you know I have some money for you, and you better take it and buy you a new pair."

"No, Bob, I will never take that except as a last resort. While I have my health I shall not allow myself to accept charity. I am not afraid to do any sort of work, and sooner or later I am confident that

HERBERT RANDOLPH SHOVELING SNOW.

I shall find employment. This morning I earned seventy five cents shoveling snow from the stoops of houses. This sort of employment, however, is very uncertain, as so little snow falls here; but there are other odd jobs to be done, and I shall try and get my share of them."

"I didn't know you was doing that kind of work, Herbert," said Bob, with a deep drawn sigh. "It ain't right for a boy with your learnin' to come down to that."

"It's right for me to do anything temporarily to earn an honest penny. One who is above work cannot hope to succeed. I am here, and I am going to stay, and the best I can do is to do always the best I can, and the best I can do just at present is to be a porter, an errand boy, a boy of all work—ready for anything, and willing to do anything, always keeping my eyes open for a chance to go a step higher.

"The trouble with me now, Bob, is that I started in too elegantly at first. I commenced in a broker's office, when I should have started at the bottom, in order to know anything about the first round of the ladder. I'm at the bottom now, and it looks as if I would have to remain there long enough to learn a good deal about that position."

"I'm glad you feel that way, Herbert, for I thought you was getting discouraged," replied Bob, his face brightening up.

"I did feel utterly discouraged for the first two or three weeks; but you know, Bob, one can get used to anything, and I have become sufficiently accustomed to this miserable kind of work, and to the beggarly pennies I earn from time to time, so that it is less cutting to me than at first. I try to content myself with the belief that it will be better by and by, though I get heart sick sometimes. It seems almost useless to try farther for work in any well established business."

The foregoing will give a very slight idea of the struggle young Randolph made to keep his head above water, and it presents a pretty true picture of the difficulties a boy will ordinarily encounter in attempting to make his way unaided in a great city like New York. Of course difficulties vary in character and severity; but it would not be safe for the average boy to expect to find less than those that surrounded our hero. Some would be more fortunate, while others would be less favored. Herbert Randolph was especially fortunate in meeting Bob Hunter, whose friendship proved as true as steel. What would have become of him while in the hands of old Gunwagner, but for Bob's effort to rescue him? And, again, how could he have fought away despondency during his enforced idleness had he lived by himself in a cold and cheerless room? Brave and manly as he was, he owed much to his warm hearted companion, whose presence and sympathy revived his drooping and almost crushed spirits.

As the days passed by, Herbert Randolph turned his attention to the most practical purposes. He almost entirely gave up looking for a steady situation, and devoted his time to doing whatever odd jobs he could hit upon that would bring him in a little money. Among the many kinds of humble employment to which he bent his energies was that of working the hoist. In New York the tall warehouses, those not supplied with an elevator, have a windlass at the top, to which is attached a heavy rope, that passes down through a wide opening to the ground floor. This rope, with a large iron hook at the end, is attached to heavy cases, or whatever is to be taken to any of the upper lofts. Another rope, passing over a big wheel, when pulled turns the windlass. This winds the main rope around it, and thus draws it up, taking with it its load, whatever that may be.

Perhaps no harder or less poetic work to an educated boy could be found than this; yet Herbert Randolph did not hesitate to throw off his coat, and work with an aching back and smarting hands as few porters would do.

He worked faithfully and honestly, with no hope of reward other than the money he would earn by his labor. And yet this very employment—this humble porter work—opened up to him an opportunity of which he had never dreamed—suggested to him an idea that he never before thought of.

It came about in this way. One day, after he had toiled for two hours or so on the hoist, and had finished his work, he went up to the cashier to get his money, as he had done many times before. A man with a satchel strapped to his shoulder was just ahead of him.

"Good morning, Mr. Smith," said the man with the satchel, addressing the cashier.

"Good morning," responded the latter. "I am glad

HERBERT RANDOLPH WORKING ON THE HOIST.

you came today, Mr. Woodman, for we have an unusually large supply of stamps on hand."

"The market is very much overstocked at present," replied Woodman, unslinging his satchel, and resting it on the desk. "I bought a thousand dollars' worth of stamps yesterday from one party at five per cent off."

"Five per cent," repeated the cashier, arching his eyebrows.

"Yes, five per cent."

"And you expect to buy from us at that rate?"

"I wish I could pay you more, but my money is all tied up now—the market is glutted, fairly glutted."

"I should think it would be, when you buy them in thousand dollar lots."

"Well, that does seem like a large amount of stamps, but I know of one lot—a ten thousand dollar lot—that I could buy within an hour, if I had the money to put into them."

"You could never get rid of so many, Woodman," said the cashier, surprised at the broker's statement.

"Oh, yes, I could work them off sooner or later, and would get par for most of them too."

"How do you do it?"

"I put them up in small lots of fifty cents and a dollar, and upwards, and sell them to my customers. Of course, when I buy big lots I do a little wholesaling, but I put away all I cannot sell at the time."

"They are sure to go sooner or later, I suppose," said the cashier.

"Oh, yes, sure to sell. During the summer months very few stamps come into the market."

"And this gives you an opportunity to work off your surplus stock?"

"Yes."

"I presume you sell as a rule to stores and business offices."

"Yes; I have a regular line of customers who buy all of their stamps off me—customers that I worked up myself."

"And they prefer buying of you to going to the post office for their supply?"

"Certainly; for I give them just as good stamps, and by buying of me they save themselves the trouble of going to the post office for them."

Herbert Randolph was waiting for his money, and overheard this conversation between the cashier and the stamp broker. He made no effort to hear it, for it did not relate to him. They spoke so loud, however, that he caught every word distinctly, and before they had finished talking the idea flashed across his mind that he would try his hand at that business. Mr. Woodman, as good fortune willed it for young Randolph, could take only a portion of the stamps the cashier wished to dispose of. When the broker had completed his purchase and gone, Herbert stepped up to the cashier for the money due him for working on the hoist. Mr. Smith handed it to him cheerfully, with a pleasant remark, which gave young Randolph an opportunity to talk with him about the stamp brokerage idea that had set his brain on fire.

"How much capital have you?" asked the cashier, with growing interest.

"With the money you just paid me I have three dollars and seventy five cents," answered Herbert, his face coloring.

The cashier smiled.

"And you think you could become a broker on that capital?" said he, with mingled surprise and amusement.

"I think I could try it on that capital if you would sell me the stamps," replied Herbert, with such intelligent assurance that he interested the cashier.

"You can certainly have the stamps," answered the latter, "and I will aid you in every way possible, but ——" and there was an ominous pause, as if thinking how he could best discourage the boy from such an undertaking.

Herbert divined his thoughts, and said, "I know such an idea must seem foolish to you, who handle so much money; but to me ——"

"Yes, you may be right, young man," interrupted the cashier. "You certainly interest me. I like ambition and pluck, and you evidently have both. When would you like the stamps?"

"Thank you," said Herbert, in a tone that lent strength to his words. "You may give them to me now, if you please—three dollars' worth. I may need the seventy five cents before I succeed in selling any stamps."

"It is a wise precaution to avoid tying up all your capital in one thing," laughed the cashier, while counting out the stamps. "They will cost you two dollars and eighty five cents, at five per cent discount, the same as I gave Mr. Woodman."

When the transaction had been completed, young Randolph left the office hurriedly, anxious to learn what the possibilities of his new undertaking were.

Ten times during that first day did he return to Mr. Smith for stamps, and ten times was his supply exhausted by customers to whom he sold at par—resulting in a profit of a dollar and fifty cents—an income that to him was a small fortune.

That night Herbert Randolph joined Bob Hunter with brighter eyes and more buoyant spirits than he had known since Mr. Goldwin's failure, now nearly three months ago.

CHAPTER XXVIII.

IN BUSINESS FOR HIMSELF.

ONLY strong characters are able to lift themselves out of poverty and adversity by sheer force of will, unaided by any one. Such a character Herbert Randolph proved himself to be. For nearly three months he had faced the most discouraging prospects. With education, with a knowledge of accounts, with splendid intelligence, with manly pride and noble ambition, he went from luxurious banking apartments to the cold wintry streets, down, down the cheerless and grim descent, till he reached the bottom, where he found himself in competition with the dregs of humanity—one of them, as far as his employment went. Imagine this proud spirited boy humbled to the degree of bidding side by side for work with a ragged Italian, a broken down and blear eyed drunkard, a cruel faced refugee from the penitentiary, or a wretched, unkempt tramp. How his young, brave heart must have ached as he found himself working on the hoist or in the street with loathsome characters of this sort—characters that purity and self respect could only shun as a pestilence.

But this he was forced to do—either this, or to acknowledge his city career a failure, and return home with crushed spirits and shattered pride, a disappointment to his father and mother and the butt of rude rural jokes for his more or less envious neighbors.

The latter is just what most boys would have done, but not so young Randolph. His eyes were closed to any such escape from his present wretched condition. Herein he showed his superior strength. But how little he realized, as he worked with dogged determination at these cheerless tasks, that this very employment would lead him into the light, as it ultimately did. Boys see nothing but drudgery in such employment, or in any humble position. They want to commence work at something genteel. An easy clerical position like the one young Randolph had with Mr. Goldwin appeals strongly to their taste. Fine clothes, white hands, little work and short hours—these are in great demand among boys. Young Randolph, indeed, was no exception to the rule. He sought a position in a bank and got it. Fortunately for him, however, the bank failed, and he was thrown into the streets. But for this he would have been a clerk still—a little three dollar machine, which bears no patent, and possesses no especial value over the ten thousand other machines capable of performing similar work. His dream of wealth and position would in all probability never have materialized. He would doubtless have in time become a head clerk at a respectable salary. But how little this would have satisfied his ambition! His desire to be at the head of the firm could never have been realized, for he would not have had the money to place himself there. The result would have been clerking, clerking, miserable, aimless clerking, and nothing more. But now, through what seemed to him his misfortune had come good fortune—through the drudgery of the hoist had come a business of his own—a growing, paying, business—*a business of great possibilities.* The suffering he had undergone did him no permanent harm. On the contrary it enabled him to appreciate more keenly the opportunity he now had for making money and supplying himself with the necessaries, and some of the luxuries, of life.

Young Randolph's brokerage business grew day by day as he added new customers and learned how to manage it more successfully. In a little time he saw the necessity of having a place where his customers could reach him by mail or messenger. He therefore arranged with a party on Nassau Street to allow him desk room. Then followed this card:

HERBERT RANDOLPH,

111 NASSAU STREET,

BUYS AND SELLS
ALL KINDS OF FOREIGN COIN AND PAPER.
United States Silver and Postage
Stamps a Specialty.

NEW YORK.

It was with much pleasure that he studied these neatly printed cards. The first thing he did after receiving them from the printer was to inclose one in a letter to his mother. He had already written her glowing accounts of his growing business, and he felt that this card would give a realism to his pen pictures that he had been unable to impart. He thought long and with pride how sacredly that little bit of pasteboard would be treasured by his parents—how proudly they would show it to their neighbors, and the comments that it would bring forth.

Then he took one over to Bob Hunter, who exhibited no little surprise as he read it admiringly.

Later in the evening he and the newsboy went as usual to visit Tom Flannery, who now, poor boy, seemed to be yielding to that dread disease—consumption. How his face brightened up as he looked at the card with scarcely less pride than if it had been his own!

"I wish I could get into that business, Herbert, when I get well," said he, turning the card languidly in his thin, emaciated fingers; "you'n' me'n' Bob. Yes, I would like that, for we always had such good times together, didn't we, Bob?"

"Yes, we did, Tom," answered Bob, tenderly. "I guess as good times as anybody ever had, even if we didn't have much money."

"So I think, Bob. I've thought of it a good many times while I've been sick here—of the detective business and all, and how grand you managed the whole thing. But then you always done everything grand, Bob. None er the boys could do it like you."

"You do some things much better than I could, Tom," said Bob.

"No, Bob. I never could do nothing like you."

"You bear your sickness more patiently than I could, and that is harder to do than anything I ever did," replied Bob.

"Well, I have to do it, you know, Bob. There ain't no other way, is there, Herb——"

The last part of the word was lost in violent coughing that racked the boy's feeble frame terribly.

"I am afraid you are talking too much, Tom," said Herbert. "We must not allow you to say any more at present."

Ten days later, and Tom had grown too weak to be dressed. Part of the time he lay bolstered up in bed, but even this taxed his strength too heavily. He had become very much wasted, and was little more than a skeleton. All hope of his recovery had been given up, and it was now simply a question of how long he could be kept alive. Bob and Herbert brought him choice fruits, and drew liberally from their slender purses to buy for him whatever would tend to make him more comfortable or would gratify his fancy.

Poor Mrs. Flannery was almost overcome with sorrow as she saw her boy wasting away and sinking lower and lower as each day passed by. He was her only child, and she loved him with all the force of her great mother's heart.

At length the end came. Bob and Herbert were present with the grief stricken mother, trying to comfort her and struggling to repress the sorrow each felt at the close approach of death.

For several hours the sick boy had been in a sort of stupor from which it seemed probable that he would never rally. He lay like one dead, scarcely breathing. Towards midnight, however, he opened his eyes and looked upon the three tear stained faces beside his bed. An expression of deepest pity settled upon his countenance, and he spoke with much effort, saying:

"Don't cry, mother; don't feel so bad for me. You have Bob and Herbert left. They will look out for you when I am gone," whispered the dying boy faintly, and he turned his eyes for confirmation to the friend who had never failed him.

"Yes," answered Bob, pressing the sufferer's hand warmly. "We will do everything you could wish us to for your mother—you would have done it for either of us, Tom."

The latter's eyes moistened and grew bright with a feeling of joy at this assurance from Bob—this last proof of his true friendship.

"I knew it before, mother," he said, nerving himself for the effort, "but it makes me happy to hear him say it before you —to hear him say it before I go."

"And you may rely upon me also, Tom, to join Bob in doing for your mother whatever would please you most," said Herbert, unable to keep back the hot tears.

"Yes, I am sure of that, Herbert. You and Bob are just alike, and can do more than I could if I had lived. I am so glad I knew you, Herbert," continued the dying boy, his face flushing with momentary animation as he recalled the past. "What good times we have had, you and me and Bob! I thought they would last always, but—but—well I wish I might have lived to go into business with you. I would have tried my best to please you, and——"

"What is it?" asked Herbert, noticing the sufferer's hesitation.

"I was going to ask you if the business, your new business, wouldn't get big enough to take Bob in with you—to make him a partner, so he can make a lot of money, too. I was almost afraid to ask you, but——"

"That is already fixed," said Bob hoarsely, almost overcome by the solicitude of his dying friend. "Herbert gave me an interest in the business today, and I shall commence working with him as soon as I am needed."

"I am so glad, so glad," responded the sufferer faintly, and with a smile that told plainly the joy this knowledge gave him. "It's all right now," he continued slowly, and with greater effort, for the little strength he had left was fast leaving him. "You will be taken care of, mother, and Bob will be taken care of by Herbert," he went on, sinking into a half unconscious state. "I know they will do well and will make rich men and have everything in the world that they want. I wish I could see them then with a big banking house and clerks and private offices and errand boys and electric bells and fine carriages and horses and a brown stone house in the avenue, may be."

TOM FLANNERY'S DEATHBED.

In a little while he regained full consciousness as if by a powerful effort, and said in a faint whisper :

"There is one thing more, mother—my knife, my little brass knife."

Mrs. Flannery brought it and placed it in his thin hands.

He looked at it with such a strange expression of affection —a little well worn knife of inexpensive make. How long he had carried it in his pocket, how many times he had held it in his hand, and now—yes, now, he held it for the last time— only this little knife, yet his all, his only legacy.

"You won't want it, will you, mother?" said he, with moist eyes and struggling with emotion.

"No, no, Tommy," sobbed the broken hearted mother.

"I knew you wouldn't," said he, "for I want to give it to Bob. It ain't much, I know, Bob," he continued, addressing the latter; "but it's all I have. You will keep it, won't you, to remember me by? When you get to be a man—a rich business man with fine offices and a house of your own, look at this knife sometimes—my knife, and think of me, and how we used to work together. Yes, you will do so, won't you, Bob?"

"I will, Tom, I will," answered Bob, as he took the little knife into his own hands. "I will keep it always to remind me of you," and he bowed his head upon the bed beside his dying friend and cried with sincere grief.

"It's all right now," responded the sufferer. "All right," he repeated, as his mother pressed her lips to his forehead.

"All right," again, so feebly that the last word fainted half spoken by his dying lips.

In a few moments the last death struggle was over. He was gone, poor Tom, the honest, trustful boy with a pure heart and noble friendship—cut off in the morning of his life by a sickness brought on by exposure, and an exposure made necessary that he might earn the means to supply his humble wants. A cruel world this seems sometimes, when one reflects how unevenly the joys and sorrows, and luxuries and misery are distributed among brothers and sisters, neighbors and countrymen.

CHAPTER XXIX.

TOM FLANNERY'S FUNERAL.

THE grief of the broken hearted mother and the two faithful friends can better be imagined than described. Words, however ably chosen, fail utterly to picture the sufferings of the human heart. In imagination we can see the three bending over the still form of him to whose heart each was attached so firmly. One, a well aged woman, still clinging passionately to the cold hands and moaning with almost frantic grief. Now she presses the lifeless figure to her breast, appealing wildly to it to speak to her, to call her "mother" just once more. Again she falls upon her knees and prays as only one prays with bursting heart, that her boy, her Tom, her only child, her very life, may be restored to her. With her tears are mingled those of Herbert and Bob, whose young spirits overflow with sorrow, not alone for their own loss at the hands of death but at the wild, tumultuous grief of the bereaved mother.

A little later we see the undertaker arrive with all his dread paraphernalia, then the casket, a plain, neat one purchased by Herbert and Bob, in due time receives the dead body.

The funeral follows speedily, and is held in Mrs. Flannery's rooms. In one of them she lies in bed helplessly ill from grief and utter prostration. All preparations for the burial have been made by Herbert and Bob. The minister arrives, and after a hurried talk with Herbert devotes himself to Mrs. Flannery, trying to lessen her sorrow by such words of consolation and assurance as his calling enables him to speak with something like holy authority.

A tall, fine looking man with a young, sweet faced girl now knocks at the door. They are Mr. Goldwin and his daughter, and the latter brings a cross of flowers for a burial offering. How strangely out of place they seem in these small, barely furnished attic rooms, yet they have come with honest purpose to pay honor to the humble dead. Mr. Goldwin had known of Tom's brave part in rescuing Herbert from the villains by whom he had been imprisoned. He had at that time sent him a reward, and now he came sorrowfully to mingle his tears with those of the lowly friends of the dead. Ray had begged to come with him, and he was glad to grant her the request, for he felt that she would receive a lesson from this simple funeral such as could not be learned elsewhere.

A delegation of newsboys about the age of the dead now arrived. They had known him well as a rival trader, as a true friend and agreeable companion. They had often asked after him during his illness, and now they came, their bright young faces heavy with sorrow, to follow his remains to the tomb. They brought with them a handsome wreath of flowers bearing the simple word "Tom."

The casket was carried into the sick room and placed on a table not far from the bed on which Mrs. Flannery lay sobbing. When all had been seated, the minister rose and prayed, such a prayer as is seldom offered. The occasion was an inspiration to the holy man. In all his years of ministry he had never been called upon to attend such a funeral as this—so simple, so strange, and yet so genuinely sad. It was a boy's funeral, and the audience was composed almost wholly of boys. The casket had been bought by boys, the details of the funeral had been arranged by boys, and boys—nearly a score of them—were there to mourn the loss of their friend. And they were no ordinary boys, with careless, thoughtless manners, but sturdy lads who were almost men in thought, for long, long months had they, like the deceased, had to think and act for themselves.

Mr. Goldwin and Ray, aided to some extent by a few of the boys, sang a hymn, and then the minister, after reading the Bible, gave a feeling and impressive talk that went home to the hearts of every one present. Bob and Herbert could not have felt greater sorrow had the dead been their own brother. They tried, however, to restrain their grief, as everything depended upon them, since Mrs. Flannery was now helpless.

At the close of the service all except Mrs. Flannery passed by the casket, looking for the last time upon the features of the dead boy before the lid was closed. The mother was bolstered up in bed, and the casket was lowered beside her, where she too could view the remains. The pall bearers were selected from the delegation of newsboys, as I think Tom would have wished had he expressed himself upon this point.

In a little time the casket had been placed within the hearse, and this strange funeral party started on its solemn journey to the tomb. Mr. Goldwin and Ray and Herbert and Bob occupied the carriage of chief mourners—not that the two former could strictly be called mourners, but their object in going to the tomb was to comfort the two boys, for whose conduct Mr. Goldwin had the greatest admiration.

The newsboys followed in other carriages, which had been secured by Bob Hunter without cost, when it was known for what purpose they were wanted.

TOM FLANNERY'S FUNERAL.

The remains of the dead boy were buried beside those of his father and sister in Greenwood Cemetery, where his mother had bought a plot at the death of her husband.

"We must buy a stone, Herbert, for Tom's grave when we can get the money," said Bob, as they came slowly away from the cemetery.

"Yes, we will do that some time, Bob," answered Herbert, with swollen eyes. "But our first duty is to take care of his mother."

"Yes, we promised him that we would look after her, and we must do it—he would have done it for either of us," answered Bob, choking with emotion as his mind went back to the death scene.

"I wish I could help do something for Mrs. Flannery, poor woman," said Ray, addressing her father.

"I shall be very glad to have you do anything in reason, my dear," replied Mr. Goldwin with pleasure. "Nothing would make me more proud of my daughter than to see her helping others who need encouragement and assistance."

"You shall be proud of me then, father," replied Ray with enthusiasm. "I am so glad you took me with you today. It has given me a new idea of life. Now I feel as if I could be of some use in the world."

RAY READING TO MRS. FLANNERY.

"You certainly can if you wish to do good, for the competition in that line is not so great as it should be," answered Mr. Goldwin thoughtfully.

"It looks so in Mrs. Flannery's case surely," remarked Herbert; "there were few to help her in her terrible trouble."

"Did she have no friends but you and Mr. Hunter?" asked Ray.

"No, I think not," answered young Randolph, "at least none that I know of."

"What would she have done, poor woman, but for your kindness?"

"I do not like to think about it," replied Herbert with a shudder.

"I think I know of a good woman who would go down and take care of Mrs. Flannery while she is sick," said Mr. Goldwin. "She certainly needs good nursing for the present."

"I wish such a woman could be had," said Herbert, "for both Bob and myself are anxious to get to work."

CHAPTER XXX.

IN A NEW HOME.

THREE weeks after the funeral Mrs. Flannery had sufficiently recovered her strength so that she could safely be moved from the rooms she had occupied so long Ray Goldwin had done much towards bringing about this satisfactory result by her frequent visits and cheerful manner—always saying and doing the right thing with admirable tact. She became much interested in the childless woman whose heart still bled unceasingly for her "poor Tom, poor Tom," as she murmured often to herself.

At the funeral Ray had contrasted her own life with that of Herbert and Bob. As she pondered over what these two humble boys, with so slender means, had done for the dying lad and his grief stricken mother, she felt how much she suffered by the comparison.

The solemnity of the occasion and the glowing words of praise for the two friends of the dead, spoken with such peculiar force by the minister, led her, as was natural, to overestimate their worth and to undervalue her own. With the same spirit, therefore, with which she admired Herbert and Bob for their acts, she condemned her own inactivity, and there in that little room beside the remains of the humble newsboy she resolved that she would be something more than a society girl as her life had hitherto been tending. She had learned a valuable lesson and given place to a purpose as noble as it was humane.

That she was carrying out this purpose her kind acts and words of comfort to Mrs. Flannery amply attested. She, however, was not alone the source of comfort while on these missions of

MRS. FLANNERY AND THE TWO BOYS IN THEIR NEW HOME.

noble charity, for the sick woman gave her, unconsciously, to be sure, as she talked of Herbert Randolph, a taste of happiness of a finer and sweeter character than she herself, poor woman, could ever hope again to feel. It was born of hero worship—a worship ripening into simple, childlike sentiment. I say hero worship, for such her thoughts of young Randolph and Bob Hunter were when she first realized how kind and generous they had been to him who now lay dead, and to his helpless and heart broken mother.

Such thoughts, however, to a young girl just verging upon the age of woman, and when the hero is a noble, manly boy like Randolph, are but the buds of the more beautiful and fragrant flower which time is sure to bring forth.

And this is the way that Ray came to find such pleasure in the simple talk of Mrs. Flannery—talk that but for this magnetic interest must have been unbearably dull to her young ears.

Herbert and Bob, feeling that it would be better for the bereaved mother to get away from her present rooms where she was constantly reminded of the dead, leased a neat little flat in Harlem, to which she was moved, together with her furniture. Here they designed making a home for themselves, inaugurating Mrs. Flannery as housekeeper. It seemed to them that they could in no other way carry out so fully the wishes of their dead friend. The housework would occupy her mind and keep her busy, and by their living thus together she would have with her the two friends in whose care the deceased had placed her. Moreover each desired a better home than their cheerless attic room had been to them, and they felt that they could now afford to spend more upon themselves.

Thus the flat was taken and with Mrs. Flannery's furniture,

a few new things from the store and little fancy articles made and contributed by Ray and her mother, the boys found themselves very happily situated in their new home. Mrs. Flannery, too, while at her new duties, recovered more quickly than would seem possible from the terrible shock she had sustained. In young Randolph and Bob Hunter she found all she could have desired in sons of her own—found, as her poor dying boy had said, that they would look out for her, and could do more for her than he. And she proved a good mother to them, studying their every want with gratitude and affection.

To Bob especially the comforts of his present life gave great happiness, and as the weeks rolled by he became more and more attached to his new home, and spent all the spare time possible in study, being taught by Herbert.

CHAPTER XXXI.

THE BOY BROKER.

WHILE young Randolph was away from his business during the few days of the death and burial of his friend, the proprietor of a house from whom Herbert bought a great many stamps complained to his bookkeeper about the large supply on hand.

"But we cannot get rid of them if no one calls for them," replied the latter.

"Hasn't Littlewood been in for any?"

"No, he has not been here for ten days."

"Ten days," repeated the merchant thoughtfully. "What has become of the boy broker? I have not seen him here lately."

"The boy broker," said the bookkeeper, taking Herbert's card from a drawer to find his address. "He is at 111 Nassau Street. Shall I send for him?"

"Yes, do so," said the proprietor as he walked away.

"The boy broker," repeated the bookkeeper to himself, catching at his employer's words. "That has a good ring to it and would sound well on young Randolph's cards."

Having a pen in his hand he dipped it in red ink and printed diagonally across Herbert's card the words THE BOY BROKER. "That looks well," said he to himself, holding it off and eying it critically. "It is catchy. I will suggest to young Randolph that he adds it to his cards and prints it in red ink as I have done. There's nothing like advertising," he went on, talking to himself. "It pays, and this will pay Randolph—I know it will."

The suggestion was accordingly made to Herbert and he adopted it, having his cards printed precisely as the one the bookkeeper had shown him.

And this is the way he became known as THE BOY BROKER. The name proved "catchy," as the bookkeeper had predicted, and after adopting it Herbert found his business growing more rapidly than ever. But just now a most unexpected bit of good luck came to the young Vermonter and at a time too when he felt sorely the need of money. The cause brought by Mr. Goldwin's lawyer against Christopher Gunwagner for false imprisonment of Herbert Randolph had come up for trial. Herbert and Bob were summoned to court to testify against the old fence.

The trial was ably conducted on both sides, but the fact that young Randolph had been restrained from his liberty by one Christopher Gunwagner, a notorious fence, was quickly established. It only remained then for the jury to find the damages.

Herbert had sued for one thousand dollars, and his lawyer made an able argument to recover the full amount.

He dwelt at length upon our hero's sufferings in that damp, musty cellar, infested as it was by rats to such a degree as to threaten his reason; all of which was only too true. Graphically did the lawyer picture this scene, so graphically that the hearts of the jurymen were noticeably touched.

Then the lawyer argued that outside and beyond the actual

injury suffered, there should be an exemplary damage awarded. The worst traits of the old fence were shown up, and contrasted with the spotless character of Herbert Randolph.

The judge in his charge sustained the idea of exemplary damage, and then the case went to the jury.

They had remained out about three quarters of an hour, when they came in and announced a verdict in favor of Herbert Randolph of *five hundred and seventy five dollars!*

Young Randolph was never more surprised in his life, or only once; and that was when he found Bob Hunter at old Gunwagner's on the night of his escape.

"Five hundred and seventy five dollars!" said he to himself, unable to realize that he had been awarded such a sum of money.

Bob Hunter congratulated him, his lawyer congratulated him, and the court even did likewise.

But none were more hearty and genuine in their congratulations than Mr. Goldwin and his pretty daughter Ray.

"I owe it all to you, Mr. Goldwin," said Herbert, gratefully. "I should never have thought to commence action against old Gunwagner but for your advice."

The odd seventy five dollars paid the lawyer and all the court expenses. This left a clear five hundred dollars for young Randolph—what a lot of money, five hundred dollars in new, crisp bank notes!

"And it shall all go into our business, Bob," said he, proudly, "and as you are now an equal partner with me half of the money will be yours."

"Oh, no, Herbert, that would not be right," protested Bob.

"Yes, I am sure it would," replied The Boy Broker. "My being imprisoned was due to no effort of my own, but rather to my simplicity, my lack of keenness. My release, on the other hand, was due to your brave efforts to rescue me. I walked into the trap unconsciously, you walked into it with your eyes open, risking your very life to save me. To you therefore the greater reward is due—you earned your portion, I helplessly endured the misery that has brought me mine."

"But I did not suffer any and you did," returned Bob, feeling keenly his helplessness when in an argument with young Randolph.

"You, however, took the chances of suffering, and those who take great chances in business, in war and in dangerous enterprises, of whatever character, if successful are well rewarded for the part they have borne. No, Bob, I would not think of keeping all this money," continued Herbert, impressively. "We are partners in business together. Let us start with equal interest, then we should feel no jealousy toward each other. This five hundred dollars will enable us to do five times the business we are now doing, and if we save the profits we make we can still further increase it month by month."

"Do you remember, Herbert," said Bob, with grateful expression, "that when Mr. Goldwin failed and you were thrown out of work I urged you to take some money—only eight dollars—and you refused it?"

"Yes, I remember it well, Bob," replied young Randolph.

"And now you ask me to take two hundred and fifty dollars from you. Why should I not refuse your offer as you refused mine?"

"Bob," said Herbert, taking him by the hand, "that eight dollars was a reserve fund, it was all that stood between you and me and starvation or what is almost as bad—public charity. I appreciated as you little knew your generous offer, and it cut me to see how hurt you felt at my refusal to take the money. But I thought of the possibility of sickness or accident, and realized how much help those few dollars would prove in such a time. Again I felt that the money would do me no good. I know now that it would not have, for I should simply have used it up and would then have been no nearer, if so near, solving the problem that pressed me for an answer—namely, how to earn sufficient means with which to buy bread and procure a shelter for myself."

"I think you were right, Herbert," replied Bob, thoughtfully. "I couldn't think so then, however, but it is plain to me now."

"I know I was right. It was the suffering I went through in those dreary winter months and the miserable drudgery I was forced to perform that at last gave me a knowledge of this business. It was an education to me, Bob, of a most practical character, and now that it is all over I can only feel glad that I was forced out of my comfortable clerkship into the cold wintry street that had so sunny an ending."

CHAPTER XXXII.

THE CONSPIRATORS' FATE.

A FEW weeks after the trial of Gunwagner for false imprisonment he was again brought before the bar of justice to answer with Felix Mortimer to the charge of conspiring to kidnap Herbert Randolph. Able counsel were employed by the old villain, and a hard fight was made for liberty. But the charges were so well sustained by the evidence of Herbert and Bob, and that of the small boy who aided the latter in gaining admittance to the fence's den, that the jury brought in a verdict of guilty.

Gunwagner was, accordingly, sentenced to serve a long term of imprisonment at Sing Sing as a penalty for his villainous acts. He had accumulated much money by crooked means, and now towards the end of his life his own freedom was the price paid for the gold which now was valueless to him.

Then came Felix Mortimer's turn. But for him Herbert Randolph would never have fallen into the trouble that seemed to await him on his arrival in New York. Young Mortimer, however, overreached himself. He was not a match for Herbert Randolph and Bob Hunter together—neither he nor all of his disreputable cronies.

His plans miscarried wofully, and now, after many long weary days of confinement in the Tombs, he found himself sentenced to the House of Correction for nearly four years, or until he reached the age of his majority.

Felix Mortimer was splendidly endowed by nature for a brilliant man. He had great ability, and was unusually bright and prepossessing. But unfortunately for him, and for the community in which he lived, he commenced life in the wrong way. He failed to recognize the fact that no true success can be attained except by operating on the solid principles of truth and honesty. His envy of Herbert Randolph had at last brought him disgrace and humiliation, while the young Vermonter now had a well paying and fast growing business of his own. How bitterly he must have regretted his own foolish and evil acts, when he realized fully to what they had brought him!

GUNWAGNER IN PRISON.

He could look now upon Herbert Randolph and say to himself, truthfully, "I had the ability to succeed as well as you have and to be as much respected as you now are. My advantages, too, were superior to yours, and yet here am I a prisoner in the House of Correction, deprived of my liberty and in disgrace, while you have already entered upon a splendid business career. And all this difference comes from my having made a wrong start."

Alas! how many human wrecks scattered all along the pathway of life could say the same thing, as they compare their present wretched condition with that of the prosperous and honored citizens—the solid men of the community—who were once their schoolfellows, and whose early career was perhaps less promising than their own. And all this difference, or nearly all, has grown naturally out of the right or wrong start they took in life.

Peter Smartweed alone among the conspirators remains to be accounted for, and this is something that the police could not do. They made a careful search throughout the city for him, but his presence could not be discovered. It was believed that, fearing arrest, he had suddenly left his home and the city in which he had spent his life, when he learned of the fate of Felix Mortimer, his companion in crime.

CHAPTER XXXIII.

A GLIMPSE AT THE FUTURE.

IT has not seemed to me desirable to dwell upon Mr. Goldwin's business affairs—to show the legal squabbles that followed his failure, or to picture in detail the trickery of Breakwell & Co. My aim has been to introduce only what bore directly upon the career of Herbert Randolph. I will say, however, that the banker's failure did not leave him penniless, as young Randolph feared it might. He was badly crippled at first, but certain securities turned over to him by Breakwell & Co., which at the time of the failure possessed but little market value, began at the end of a few months to advance rapidly. When they had reached a point at which it seemed to him advisable to sell he closed them out at a price that enabled him to pay off all his obligations without drawing upon his personal property for a penny. He was, therefore, still a wealthy man, and was not forced to reduce his style of living in the slightest degree.

With this simple statement I leave the past to record a conversation in which the reader will catch a glimpse of the future, in so far as it relates to some of those who have been most conspicuous in this story.

Young Randolph had now become a frequent visitor at Mr. Goldwin's home, where, notwithstanding the many attractions of a great city, he spent the happiest hours of his life. Bob Hunter, moreover, was not an entire stranger at this handsome residence. His visits, though, were few in comparison to those of his partner, and this was due to two causes—first, a decided reluctance to leave his books, for he had become a most industrious student, and second, the lack of so delightful an attraction as that which turned the steps of the young Vermonter so often towards the Goldwin home.

It was now midwinter. Herbert and Bob had been in business together nearly nine months, in which time they had by hard work and splendid ability lifted themselves from poverty and drudgery to a position of prosperity. In an up town savings bank a snug sum of money was deposited to their credit, and this was in excess of the amount used in their business, which had become so large that a good working capital was necessary.

One day they received a letter from Mr. Goldwin inviting them to dine with him and his family on the following evening. The letter stated, moreover, that he wished to talk with them about a matter in which he thought they would feel an interest.

"What can he wish to talk over with us?" said Bob.

"I have been speculating on that same point," replied Herbert.

"And you came to no conclusion?"

"No, I really cannot imagine his purpose."

"It may be about business," suggested the junior partner.

"You may be right, Bob, but it hardly seems probable that he would want to talk with us about business."

"But you say he has often talked with you about it when you have been at his house."

"So he has, in a general way," replied Herbert, "but I supposed that was just to fill in conversation."

"A mere matter of curiosity to know how we were doing?"

"Yes."

"It's possible, though, that he had other objects in view."

"Possible, well, yes; but not probable."

Thus the boys speculated upon Mr. Goldwin's purpose, as they went about their work—speculated and wondered till they found themselves at his table, where all thought of this character was driven from their minds by the pleasant conversation that followed.

It was only fifteen months before this that two boys met as if by chance in City Hall Park one brisk October morning—one a country lad fresh from the rocky hills of old Vermont, the other a keen eyed, bright faced newsboy of New York. Look at the group around this table, and tell me if you can see these chance acquaintances—the boy whose every act proclaimed him a farmer's son, or the other—the shabbily dressed product of a metropolitan street. And if perchance by voice or feature you recognize the boy of education and ambition, look again, I urge you, that you may find his friend. "There is but one boy present beside him of the farm," I hear you say, "and surely it cannot be he, so well dressed and grown so tall, whose language bespeaks a well bred lad." But look yet once more, I pray you, and behold the sparkle of his eyes, the old time humor playing over his features, and—ah! now he laughs and shows his dimples once again—the same on either cheek reflecting the merriment he feels. You yield at last, puzzled though I know you are, and the question you would put to me—"How came it so, this marvelous change in these two boys?" I will answer—THEY WORKED AND STUDIED.

BOB HUNTER, THE STUDENT AND YOUNG BUSINESS MAN.

When dinner was over Mr. Goldwin and the two boys repaired to the library. After a little preliminary talk the former said,

"I am contemplating going into business again."

"Your old business?" asked Herbert.

"Yes," replied Mr. Goldwin, rather deliberately, resting comfortably in his easy chair and toying with his eye glasses. "I am better fitted for that than any other. But my object is not wholly to make money, though of course there is always pleasure in doing so. My purpose is rather to provide myself with some light employment that would interest me, but which would not be too severe a tax upon my strength. I have also a secondary object in this connection," he continued, addressing Herbert, "and that is a desire to put you and Bob in the way of entering a first class brokerage business much sooner than you could hope to if left to your own efforts. I have watched both of you carefully and with the keenest interest. The ability you have each shown in conducting your stamp brokerage convinces me that you are capable of moving up higher, and therefore it gives me pleasure to offer you an interest in the business that I am about to start."

"But the money!" exclaimed both boys, speaking at once and almost doubting their own senses, yet expressing in their looks thanks more eloquent than words could have conveyed.

"The money question can be arranged all right," replied Mr. Goldwin. "I can supply the necessary sum in excess of your capital."

"I can hardly realize such an opportunity as open to us," said Herbert, adding words of warmest thanks.

"Neither can I," remarked Bob, no less expressive in his gratitude to Mr. Goldwin.

"Doubtless it is a surprise to you," replied the latter; "but the idea has been growing with me for several months, and now I am ready to make you this proposition. You of course know that you are not old enough to become legal partners. It will therefore be necessary to conduct the business under my own name, and as this was my old business name it will be better than a new one."

"We certainly shall not object to that," said Herbert; "but how can we become members of the firm if not legal partners?"

"You can become practically members, though not real members," returned Mr. Goldwin. "That is to say you can draw a certain percentage of the profits in return for your capital and services. My proposition then is this: I will open an office and take both of you boys in with me, allowing you one half of the profits until you become of age; then we will organize a partnership, and each own a third of the business. By that time your profits, if you do not spend too much money, will enable you to own your interests clear of all incumbrance. Your present brokerage business can be done from our office, and that I shall want Bob to attend to at first, while you, Herbert, I shall expect to bear the brunt of the burden in our regular business. Your experience with me before my failure taught you what is to be done. We will commence in a small way at first, and I shall not do very much work myself. I will of course keep an eye on everything, and may bring many of my old customers back to us. Now you have heard my proposition," continued Mr. Goldwin, "how do you like it?"

"I could not possibly like anything better," replied Herbert, "but it seems too good to be true—more like an air castle than a fact."

"So it seems to me," added Bob.

"But it is a fact," laughed Mr. Goldwin, enjoying the surprise of the two young partners, "and I am ready to start the ball rolling at once."

"We will certainly accept the proposition, then," said Herbert, speaking for himself and Bob; "which is, as I understand, that you are to draw one half of the profits, and that Bob and I will each get one quarter?"

"Yes, that is correct, up to the time you both become of age," replied Mr. Goldwin.

"After that we are to become equal partners?" said Bob.

"Yes, and of course each draw one third of the profits," returned Mr. Goldwin. "Whenever our new business," he continued, "becomes large enough to demand Bob's full time, I should advise selling the stamp department. Until then, however, we will hold it, as it pays a handsome little income which will swell our first year's profits considerably."

"Are you not ready for our game of chess, Mr. Randolph?" said Ray Goldwin, appearing in the library door.

"That depends upon your father's wishes," answered Herbert, all too anxious to join her.

"What say you, papa?" appealed Ray.

"Your wishes are law with me, my dear," said the father, with a happy smile. "Go, Herbert, and win if you can."

"But the business," suggested young Randolph, as he quickly joined Ray in the doorway.

"Ah, never mind that now; the game will suit you better, and besides Bob and I can arrange the few details yet to be talked over."

THE END.

www.ingramcontent.com/pod-product-compliance
Lightning Source LLC
Chambersburg PA
CBHW020854270326
41928CB00006B/695

* 9 7 8 3 3 3 7 0 1 5 7 2 5 *